For over a decade, The New York Public Library and Oxford University Press have annually invited a prominent figure in the arts and letters to give a series of lectures on a topic of his or her choice. Subsequently these lectures become the basis of a book jointly published by the Library and the Press. For 2002 and 2003 the two institutions asked seven noted writers, scholars, and critics to offer a "meditation on temptation" on one of the seven deadly sins. *Envy* by Joseph Epstein is the first book from this lecture series.

Previous books from The New York Public Library/Oxford University Press Lectures are:

The Old World's New World by C. Vann Woodward

Culture of Complaint: The Fraying of America by Robert Hughes

Witches and Jesuits: Shakespeare's Macbeth by Garry Wills

Visions of the Future: The Distant Past, Yesterday, Today, Tomorrow
by Robert Heilbroner

Doing Documentary Work by Robert Coles

The Sun, the Genome, and the Internet by Freeman J. Dyson

The Look of Architecture by Witold Rybczynski

Visions of Utopia by Edward Rothstein, Herbert Muschamp,
and Martin E. Marty

Also by Joseph Epstein

Envy

Pride

Michael Eric Dyson

Envy

Joseph Epstein

Anger

Robert A. F. Thurman

Sloth

Wendy Wasserstein

Greed

Phyllis Tickle

Gluttony

Francine Prose

Lust

Simon Blackburn

Envy

The Seven Deadly Sins

Joseph Epstein

The New York Public Library

OXFORD
UNIVERSITY PRESS

OXFORD
UNIVERSITY PRESS

Oxford University Press, Inc., publishes works that
further Oxford University's objective of excellence
in research, scholarship, and education.

Oxford   New York
Auckland   Cape Town   Dar es Salaam   Hong Kong   Karachi
Kuala Lumpur   Madrid   Melbourne   Mexico City   Nairobi
New Delhi   Shanghai   Taipei   Toronto

With offices in
Argentina   Austria   Brazil   Chile   Czech Republic   France   Greece
Guatemala   Hungary   Italy   Japan   Poland   Portugal   Singapore
South Korea   Switzerland   Thailand   Turkey   Ukraine   Vietnam

First published by Oxford University Press, Inc., 2003
198 Madison Avenue, New York, NY 10016
www.oup.com

First issued as an Oxford University Press paperback, 2006
ISBN-13: 978-0-19-531204-1
ISBN-10: 0-19-531204-X

The Library of Congress has cataloged the hardcover edition as follows:
Epstein, Joseph, 1937-
Envy : the seven deadly sins / Joseph Eptstein.
p. cm.
Includes bibliographical references and index.
ISBN-13: 978-0-19-515812-0
ISBN-10: 0-19-515812-1
1. Envy. I. Title.
BF575.E65E67   2003
179'.8—dc21   2003003630

All cartoons courtesy of *The New Yorker:* p. xvi © Mort Gerberg;
p. 10 © Barbara Smaller; pp. 24, 38 © Edward Koren; p. 30 © J. P. Rini;
p. 66 © J. B. Handelsman; p. 76 © Leo Cullum; p. 90 ©Al Ross.

9 8 7 6 5 4 3 2

Printed in the United States of America
on acid-free paper

To my friend Gary W. Fisher,
who has a happy deficiency of the quality that is
the subject of this book.

Contents

Editor's Note

This volume is part of a lecture and book series on the Seven Deadly Sins cosponsored by The New York Public Library and Oxford University Press. Our purpose was to invite scholars and writers to chart the ways we have approached and understood evil, one deadly sin at a time. Through both historical and contemporary explorations, each writer finds the conceptual and practical challenges that a deadly sin poses to spirituality, ethics, and everyday life.

The notion of the Seven Deadly Sins did not originate in the Bible. Sources identify early lists of transgressions classified in the 4th century by Evagrius of Pontus and then by John of Cassius. In the 6th century, Gregory the Great formulated the traditional seven. The sins were ranked by increasing severity, and judged to be the greatest offenses to the soul and the root of all other sins. As certain sins were subsumed into others and similar terms were used interchangeably according to theological review, the list evolved to include the seven as we know them: Pride, Greed, Lust, Envy, Gluttony, Anger, and Sloth. To counter these violations, Christian theologians classified the Seven Heavenly Virtues—the cardinal: Prudence, Temperance, Justice, Fortitude, and the theological: Faith, Hope, and Charity. The sins inspired Medieval and Renaissance writers including Chaucer, Dante, and Spenser, who personified the seven in rich and memorable characters. Depictions grew to include associated colors, animals, and punishments in hell for the deadly offenses. Through history, the famous list has emerged in theological and philosophical tracts, psychology, politics, social criticism, popular culture, and art and literature. Whether the deadly seven to you represent the most common human foibles or more serious spiritual shortcomings, they stir the imagination and evoke the inevitable question—what is *your* deadly sin?

Our contemporary fascination with these age-old sins, our struggle against or celebration of them, reveals as much about our continued desire to define human nature as it does about our divine aspirations. I hope that this book and its companions invite the reader to indulge in a similar reflection on vice, virtue, the spiritual, and the human.

Elda Rotor

Then, since all self-knowledge
Tempts man into envy,
May you, by acquiring
Proficiency in what
Whitehead calls the art of
Negative Prehension,
Love without desiring
All that you are not.

—W. H. Auden

"Many Happy Returns"

Pity is for the living, envy for the dead.

—Mark Twain

Preface

When I was asked about my interest in doing a book in the Oxford University Press series of books on the seven deadly sins, pride, gluttony, and greed were already spoken for. I could therefore choose among anger, sloth, lust, and envy. Gluttony, had it not been claimed, was enticing to me, a thin man in whom—to reverse Cyril Connolly's well-known remark—a fat man has long been struggling to get out. I was drawn, also, to sloth, which a nervous temperament—I am a man of the *schpilkes,* or needles-in-the-pants school of personal psychology—has never allowed me to practice in a sustained and dedicated way; and the notion of making something like a vocation of laziness, though unavailable to me in life, nonetheless seemed immensely appealing to write about. Lust, sad to report, was never in the picture. Beyond a certain age—and I fear I have reached it—too great an interest in lust appears unseemly, not to say obscene, in a man.

No, in the end, as perhaps in the beginning, I was the envy man. A friend, a psychiatrist, told me that he thought me unsuited to the subject, being, he said, among the least envious people he knew. Pleasing to think this might be so. But, as a moderately introspective fellow, I know better. I have felt

"He's certainly been getting a lot more than his normal share of media coverage lately."

enough—and more than enough—envy in my life to qualify for writing about it. Possibly there have been certain persons—saints, great natural athletes, dazzlingly beautiful women, scions of billionaires—who have not known envy, but permit me to doubt it. To err may be human, but to envy is undoubtedly so.

Although I don't wish to seem rivalrous, nonetheless among the seven deadly sins, envy, I feel, may be the most pervasive, interpenetrating as it so insidiously does the other six major sins:

greed may begin in envy; it certainly figures in lust and gluttony (one doesn't really like to see others fornicating or eating too well, does one?); it is a division of anger, if of the hidden, smoldering kind; and pride and envy are inextricable, with the wounding of one's own pride leading on to envy as surely as spite follows defeat. But I hope I am not being unduly prideful in making the claims I do for envy, my own charming little deadly sin.

Before passing on to envy itself, a word or two on the nature of the seven deadlies is perhaps in order. In the 1950s, Ian Fleming, then a member of the Editorial Board of the *London Sunday Times*, proposed a collection of seven pieces on each of the deadly sins to the editors, who readily accepted the idea. An all-star literary cavalcade of English writers was commissioned to write, all too briefly, on the various sins: Angus Wilson on envy, Edith Sitwell on pride, Cyril Connolly on covetousness, Patrick Leigh-Fermor on gluttony, Evelyn Waugh on sloth, Christopher Sykes on lust, W. H. Auden on anger. Ah, giant chroniclers of sin walked the earth in those days.

In his five-page foreword to the book, Ian Fleming says a few kind words for each of the seven traditional deadly sins, remarking, "How drab life would be without these sins, what dull dogs we all would be without a healthy trace of many of them in our makeup." He remarks, too, on the fact that literature has needed them as subject matter quite as much as the great painters have needed primary colors. He posits an updating, or a list of what he takes to be the new seven deadly sins: avarice, cruelty, snobbery, hypocrisy, self-righteousness, moral cowardice, and malice. He ends, very neatly I think, with a list of the seven deadly virtues, which, in his reckoning, include: frugality, charity (springing from self-interest), sociability, deference (when it is in danger of lapsing into sycophancy), neatness (in excess), cleanliness (when pathological), and finally chastity (as a cloak for frigidity).

As the author of a recent book on snobbery, one of Fleming's new deadly sins, and as of the moment the country's, perhaps the world's, leading snobographer, I cannot resist listing the seven deadly sins of snobbery. These are—trumpets please—serving veal and/or iceberg lettuce to company; sending one's children to land-grant colleges; admitting to having voted for George Bush, the father or the son; owning a Cadillac SUV; mocking denim in public; and openly acknowledging one's pleasure in slightly overweight women, sweet wine, and Tchaikovsky.

And yet the original seven deadly sins continue to carry a certain weight and gravity. They cannot be dispensed with. They have a place, not only in the permanent moral categories of human beings, but in literature itself. One has only to glimpse the rich tradition of aphorism and maxim writing to discover that, without the seven deadly sins, the French *moralistes* and other writers would be quite out of business.

The origins of envy, like those of wisdom, are unknown, a mystery. People confident of their religion might say envy is owing to original sin, part of the baggage checked through on the way out of the Garden of Eden. The Bible is filled with stories of envy, some acted out, many subdued. Of the essence of envy is its clandestinity, its surreptitiousness. Envy is above all the hidden emotion—so hidden that, often, one isn't aware oneself that it is, as it frequently can be, the motive for one's own conduct.

Curiously, among philosophers, those who wrote most penetratingly about envy were all bachelors: Kant, Kierkegaard, Schopenhauer, Nietzsche chief among them. Make of this datum what you will. Nietzsche said that a married philosopher was a joke. No doubt he was thinking of the world's greatest philosopher, Socrates, being dragged home—by the ear, as one pictures the scene—by his wife Xanthippe.

Small, hunchbacked, certain he would not be long-lived (and, dying at 42, he was not wrong), as Sören Kierkegaard looked about the world, he would himself seem to have had lots to envy. He chose instead to examine envy, noting, among other things, that envy seemed to be a small-town sport. He early pointed out that in a leveling society, where equality is the announced goal, envy is likely to be all the stronger. Envy, Kierkegaard wrote, "takes the form of *leveling*, and whereas a passionate age *accelerates, raises up and overthrows, elevates, and debases*, a reflective

apathetic age does the opposite, it *stifles* and *impedes, it levels.*"
But more about envy and leveling later in this book.

Immanuel Kant, on his daily walks around the city of
Königsberg, came to believe that envy was a natural impulse,
"inherent in the nature of man [and let us add, in the interest of
equal opportunity, of women], and only its manifestation makes
of it an abominable vice, a passion not only distressing and
tormenting to the subject, but intent on the destruction of the
happiness of others, and one that is opposed to man's duty
towards himself as towards other people." Envy is opposed to
oneself, in Kant's view, because it "disinclines us to see our own
good overshadowed by the good of others." Kant also saw
ingratitude as a division or department of envy, part of "the vice
of human hate that is the complete opposite of human love."

The notion of envy runs throughout Nietzsche's various
works. Nietzsche thought the French and subsequent revolu-
tions were fired by the impulse of envy. He tended to assume
that the spiritually small man envied the spiritually large. "The
golden sheath of pity conceals the dagger of envy," he wrote. He
felt that "sometimes we owe a friend to the lucky circumstance
that we give him no cause for envy." All this is perfectly
consistent with a philosopher who once wrote, "A people [by
which he meant a nation] is a detour of nature to get six or seven
great men."

My own favorite among the philosophical commentators on envy is Schopenhauer. But then I have a general weakness for Schopenhauer, who reads well even in poor translations, such was his natural power, and whose darkness is so brilliant that, after reading him—"My nights were sour," Ira Gershwin wrote, "Spent with Schopenhauer"—the rest of the world automatically seems to light up. "Man is at bottom a savage, horrible beast," Schopenhauer writes, and it is the business of civilization to tame and restrain him. The job, in Schopenhauer's steady view, is rarely brought off in a successful way. For in "the boundless egotism of our nature there is joined more or less in every human breast a fund of hatred, anger, envy, rancor, and malice, accumulated like the venom in a serpent's tooth, and waiting only an opportunity of venting itself and then, like a demon unchained, of storming and raging." Not exactly what we should nowadays call a fun guy, Schopenhauer.

But here is the Schopenhauerian catechism on envy, the short course. "Because they feel unhappy, men cannot bear the sight of someone they think is happy." Naturally and unavoidably, "a human being, at the sight of another's pleasure and possessions, would feel his own deficiency with more bitterness." He reminds us that "hatred always accompanies envy." He then goes on to report that envy is rarely felt so keenly as in relation to natural, inborn abilities and gifts in others: high intelligence, specific genius (as for music, mathematics), and beauty.

So endemic did these and other philosophers find envy, so pervasive in every society, that, after reading them, it becomes clear that one must factor in envy in considering our judgments of our own and of others' actions. If one's own judgments are to be straight and honorable, one must be certain that they are not infected by envy. To do so one must begin by understanding the mechanics of envy: what triggers it, what sustains it, what effects it can cause.

When confronted with a serious setback or unchangeable sadness in one's life, one is inclined to ask the obvious question, Why me? For the envious person, though, the question, when he or she *sees* someone who has had greater good fortune, is, Why not me? Why should this woman be more beautiful than I? Why is this man richer and more powerful? Why do these others have an abundance of natural talents and gifts not available to me? Lord Chesterfield declared that "people hate those who make them feel their own inferiority." Certainly that makes us ask, Why was I left out? Why not me?

Some occupations are more prone to envy than others, and my strong suspicion is that literature is among the most pronounced in this line. Academic life is another field heavily laden with the landmines of envy. (Perhaps my own experience in both fields makes me think this, and envy is quite as strong in quilting and sumo wrestling circles.) If you wish to smell envy in the very air, visit Harvard, Yale, Princeton, Chicago, Berkeley, or Stanford the morning after the MacArthur genius (so-called) grants are announced. In literary as in academic life, the standards for winning fame, money, and the rest are fairly shaky and hence usually in dispute, which clears the ground for envy, resentment, and spite among fellow workers in the same vineyard.

Many of William Hazlitt's aphorisms, collected under the title *Characteristics*, are about envy. "Those who are most distrustful of themselves," he writes, "are the most envious of others: as the most weak and cowardly are the most revengeful." The English novelist Arnold Bennett, after writing in his *Journal* on 1 April 1908 that "I expect that I am as happy as I can be," four weeks later notes, "Noticed in myself, a distinct feeling of jealousy [he means envy] on reading yesterday and today of another successful production of a play by Somerset Maugham—the third now running. Also, in reading an enthusiastic account of a new novelist in the *Daily News* today, I looked eagerly for any sign to show that he was not after all a first-class artist. It relieved me to find that his principal character was somewhat conventional, etc., etc." Cynthia Ozick wrote a fine story called "Envy, Or Yiddish in America," about the generation of immigrant writers who used the Yiddish language in the United States but did not get good translators and thus were precluded from any chance of winning the glittering prizes that went to Isaac Bashevis Singer. "Why Ostover [the Singerish character]?" the story's protagonist asks. "Why not someone else?"

In *Facial Justice*, a plastic surgery dystopian novel, the English novelist L. P. Hartley shows the hopelessness of a society in which no one is supposed to look any different—which is really to say, any better—than anyone else. All faces, in this novel, are, by government decree, to be the same. No one will be surprised to learn that it all breaks down. The moral of the tale is that equality is not to be had nor envy eliminated, at least in this life.

Capitalists, those of the pure free-market variety, might conclude that, on balance, envy isn't really such a bad thing. It stirs people to aspiration, incites them to buy goods: one way to keep up with the Joneses is, after all, to outbuy them. The entire advertising industry in this light can be viewed as little more than a vast and intricate envy-creating machine. Displaying all that *luxe*—those clothes, cars, jewelry, and the rest of it—advertisements suggest that all one's desires are easily within reach. They aren't, of course, but even if they were, one may be sure that one's envy would not be permitted to sleep—further advertising is there to ensure against that. Might it be that, when our backs are turned, Adam Smith's famous "invisible hand of the market" is showing us a long and bony middle finger?

"In Dreams Begin Responsibility" is the title of a Delmore Schwartz short story, a wonderful phrase that does not quite pass the test of logic, for its reverse is also true: in dreams also begin irresponsibility. Envy, I believe, begins in dreams, often in daydreams. One of the chief categories of our dreams is of things we don't have, can't have, and, it may well be, shouldn't have. Depend upon it, these are also usually things that others have. Why them? And again, as always among those of us who have known envy, Why not us? The pages that follow attempt to speculate upon the extensive ramifications of that question.

Envy

Not Jealousy

Of the seven deadly sins, only envy is no fun at all. Sloth may not seem much fun, nor anger either, but giving way to deep laziness has its pleasures and the expression of anger entails a release that is not without its small delights. In recompense, envy may be the subtlest—perhaps I should say the most insidious—of the seven deadly sins. Surely it is the one that people are least likely to want to own up to, for to do so is to admit that one is probably ungenerous, mean, small-hearted. It may also be the most endemic. Apart from Socrates, Jesus, Marcus Aurelius, Saint Francis, Mother Teresa, and only a few others, at one time or another, we have all felt flashes of envy, even if in varying intensities, from its minor pricks to its deep, soul-destroying, lacerating stabs. So widespread is it—a word for envy, I have read, exists in all known languages—that one is ready to believe it is the sin for which the best argument can be made that it is part of human nature.

Is envy a "feeling," an "emotion," a "sin," a "temperamental disposition," or a "world-view"? Might it also be a Rorschach test: tell what you envy and you reveal a great deal about yourself. It can be all of these things—and more. No one would doubt that, whatever else it is, envy is certainly a charged, indeed a super-charged, word: one of the few words left in the English language that retains the power to scandalize. Most of us could still sleep decently if accused of any of the other six deadly sins; but to be accused of envy would be seriously distressing, so clearly does such an accusation go directly to character. The other deadly sins, though all have the disapproval of religion, do not so thoroughly, so deeply demean, diminish, and disqualify a person. Not the least of its stigmata is the pettiness implicit in envy.

The *Webster's* definition of the word won't quite do: "(1) *Obs.* malice; (2) painful or resentful awareness of the advantage enjoyed by another joined with a desire to possess the same advantage." The *Oxford English Dictionary* is rather better: it defines envy first as "malignant or hostile feeling; ill-will, malice, enmity," and then as "active evil, harm, mischief," both definitions accounted *Obscure.* But the great *OED* only gets down to serious business in its third definition, where it defines envy as "the feeling of mortification and ill-will occasioned by the contemplation of superior advantages possessed by another," in which usage the word envy first pops up around 1500. It adds a fourth definition, one in which the word is used without "notions of malevolence," and has to do with the (a) "desire to equal another in achievement, or excellence; emulation," and (b) speaks to "a longing for the advantages enjoyed by another person." Aristotle, in *The Rhetoric*, writes of emulation as good envy, or envy ending in admiration, and thus in the attempt to imitate the qualities one began by envying. Yet it must be added that envy doesn't generally work this way. Little is good about envy, except shaking it off, which, as any of us who have felt it deeply knows, is not so easily done.

Both the *OED* and *Webster's* definitions are inattentive to the crucial distinction between envy and jealousy. Most people, failing to pick up the useful distinction between envy and jealousy, mistakenly use the two words interchangeably. I suspect people did not always do so. H. W. Fowler, in his splendid *Modern English Usage* of 1926, carries no entry on either word, suggesting that formerly there was no confusion. Bryan A. Garner, in his 1998 *Dictionary of American Usage*, says that "the careful writer distinguishes between these terms," but does not himself do so sufficiently. He writes that "*jealousy* is properly restricted to contexts involving affairs of the heart, *envy* is used more broadly of resentful contemplation of a more fortunate person."

With the deep pedantic delight one takes in trumping a recognized usage expert, it pleases me to say, Not quite so. The real distinction is that *one is jealous of what one has, envious of what other people have.* Jealousy is not always pejorative; one can after all be jealous of one's dignity, civil rights, honor. Envy, except when used in the emulative sense mentioned by Aristotle, is always pejorative. If jealousy is, in cliché parlance, spoken of as the "green-eyed monster," envy is cross-, squinty-, and blearily red-eyed. Never, to put it very gently, a handsome or good thing, envy.

Although between jealousy and envy, jealousy is often the more intensely felt of the two, it can also be the more realistic: one is, after all, sometimes correct to feel jealousy. And not all jealousy plays the familiar role of sexual jealousy. One may be jealous—again, rightly—of one's reputation, integrity, and other good things. One is almost never right to feel envy: to be envious is to be, *ipso facto*, wrong.

Apart from emulative envy, the only aspect of envy that does not seem to me pejorative is a form of envy I have myself felt, as I suspect have others who are reading this book: the envy that I think of as faith envy. This is the envy one feels for those who have the true and deep and intelligent religious faith that sees them through the darkest of crises, death among them. If one is oneself without faith and wishes to feel this emotion, I cannot recommend a better place to find it than in the letters of Flannery

O'Connor. There one will discover a woman still in her thirties, who, after coming into her radiant talent, knows she is going to die well before her time and, owing to her Catholicism, faces her end without voicing complaint or fear. I not long ago heard, in Vienna, what seemed to me a perfect rendering of Beethoven's *Ninth Symphony*, and was hugely moved by it, but how much more would I have been moved, I could not help wonder, if I were in a state of full religious belief, since the *Ninth Symphony* seems to me in many ways a religious work. Faith envy is envy, alas, about which one can do nothing but quietly harbor it.

Envy must also be distinguished from general yearning. One sees people at great social ease and wishes to be more like them; or feels keenly how good it would be once more to be young; or longs to be wealthier; or pines to be taller, thinner, more muscular, less awkward, more beautiful generally. All this is yearning. Envy is never general, but always very particular—at least envy of the kind one feels strongly.

The envious tend to be injustice collectors. "Envy, among other ingredients, has a love of justice in it," William Hazlitt wrote. "We are more angry at undeserved than at deserved good fortune." Something to it, but, my sense is, not all that much. Yet much more often than not envy expresses feelings more personal than the love of justice. In another useful distinction, Kierkegaard in *The Sickness unto Death* wrote that "admiration is happy self-surrender; envy is unhappy self-satisfaction." Envy asks one leading question: What about me? Why does he or she have beauty, talent, wealth, power, the world's love, and other gifts, or at any rate a larger share of them than I? Why not me?

Dorothy Sayers, in a little book on the seven deadly sins, writes: "Envy is the great leveler: if it cannot level things up, it will level them down. . . . At its best, Envy is a climber and a snob; at its worst it is a destroyer—rather than have anyone happier than itself, it will see us all miserable together." A self-poisoning of the mind, envy is usually less about what one lacks than about what other people have. A strong element of the begrudging resides in envy, thus making the envious, as Immanuel Kant remarked in *The Metaphysics of Morals,* "intent on the destruction of the happiness of others."

One might call someone or something—another's family life, health, good fortune—"enviable" without intending rancor. In the same way, one might say, "I envy you your two-month holiday in the south of France," without, in one's mind, plotting how to do the person out of it. Or one might say, "I don't envy him the responsibilities of his job," by which one merely means that one is pleased not to have another's worries. There probably ought to be a word falling between envy and admiration, as there ought to be a word that falls between talent and genius. Yet there isn't. The language is inept.

Nor ought envy to be confused with open conflict. Someone has something that one feels one wants—customers, a high ranking or rating, government office, a position of power—and one contends for it, more or less aggressively, but out in the open. The openness changes the nature of the game. Envy is almost never out in the open; it is secretive, plotting, behind the scenes. Helmut Schoeck, who in *Envy: A Theory of Social Behavior* has written the most comprehensive book on the subject of envy, notes that it "is a silent, secretive process and not always verifiable." Envy, to qualify as envy, has to have a strong touch— sometimes more than a touch—of malice behind it.

Malice that cannot speak its name, cold-blooded but secret hostility, impotent desire, hidden rancor, and spite all cluster at the center of envy. La Rochefoucauld opened the subject of envy nicely with a silver stiletto, when he wrote: "In the misfortune of our best friends, we always find something that is not displeasing to us." Yes, really not displeasing at all. Dear old envy.

CHAPTER TWO

Spotting the Envious

Connoisseurs of the deadly sins divide them into the warm-hearted or cold-blooded sins. Lust, anger, and gluttony in this reckoning are thought warm hearted, bodily sins, proceeding as they do from the physical passions; pride, greed, sloth, and envy are cold-blooded, proceeding as they do from states of mind. The cold-blooded sins are more rebukable, less forgivable, and (with the exception of sloth) inherently crueler. Envy, a case could easily enough be made, may be the cruelest of all.

How can one recognize the envious? Physically, Horace thought those who envy others themselves grow thin. Shakespeare, perhaps picking up on this point, gave us his "lean and hungry Cassius." But later J. F. Powers, in his excellent story

"I envy you—I wish I were close enough to my family to be estranged."

"Prince of Darkness," remarks upon "the fat man's contempt and envy for the thin man." It is, as they say, a wash.

A manual for spotting the envious would be most helpful. The envious often go in for irony, the art of saying one thing and meaning another. Watch out, too, for excessive scorn even when used by oneself, for as Paul Valéry says "on close inspection we find that scorn includes a spice of envy," the tendency of most people is to scorn what they cannot do or have. The envious also tend to overpraise. "Whereas true admiration keeps its distance, the distance between the admirer and the admired one," the psychiatrist Leslie Farber wrote, "envy's assault upon its object with a barrage of compliments serves not only its need to assert itself in the costume of admiration, but also the lust of the envier to possess the very quality that initially incited his envy." The moral of the story is to watch the eyes of those who bow lowest.

One might think that something akin to a psychological profile of the envious exists. Yet it is discouraging to learn, from W. Gerrod Parrott, in his contribution to a book titled *The Psychology of Jealousy & Envy*, that "on the whole, little is known about individual differences in susceptibility to envy." Why is it given to some people to feel envy only glancingly if at all, others to use envy toward emulation and hence self-improvement, and to still others to let it build a great bubbling caldron of poisoning bile in them? What makes this and so much else about envy difficult to determine is that envy is for the most part a secret sin. People do not readily confess to envy, let alone say what it is behind their envy. Leslie Farber remarked that "envy, by its very nature, is obstinate in its opposition to investigation," and its "protean character" and "its talent for disguise" probably account for "the infrequency of studies on the subject." Quite so: one can never, for example, poll people on what or whom they envy, not so long as they understand the meanness inherent in the word.

Yet entire bodies of theory exist founded on envy as normal human conduct. Freudianism is prominent among them. Think how much envy is at the center of Freudian psychology; envy is, for Freud, perhaps the chief currency in the psychic economy. Begin with the Oedipus complex, which is little more than the son's envy of the father's right to sleep with his mother. From there let us trip lightly over to the "penis envy" that all young girls and women are supposed to feel, at least till prostate cancer rolls around. At issue in sibling rivalry is envy, or the struggle to win and hold the maximum amount of love from parents. Envy seems, too, at the heart of sublimation. One pretends to want one thing when one really wants—or secretly envies—another: "The artist gives up power, money, and the love of beautiful women for his art," said Freud, "through which he hopes to win power, money, and the love of beautiful women." In the Freudian cosmos, envy, it could be said, makes the world go round.

In the psychology of Melanie Klein, envy is all about the pursuit of the child for the mother's breast, over which he prefers something like a freehold, or lifelong lease. The child wants no competitors. "It could be said," Dr. Klein writes in her paper "Envy and Gratitude," "that the very envious person is insatiable, he can never be satisfied because his envy stems from within and therefore always finds an object to focus on." The child is even envious of "the satisfactory breast. The very ease with which the milk comes—though the infant feels gratified by it—also gives rise to envy because this gift seems something unattainable." W. H. Auden once said that "the motto of psychology ought to be, 'Have you heard this one?'"

Frank J. Sulloway, in *Born to Rebel: Birth Order, Family Dynamics, and Creative Lives*, a book about the importance of birth order within families, holds that sibling competition for the love of the parents assigns us not only our personalities, but also our politics and possibly even our sexual orientation. Sulloway feels that, "depending on differences in birth order, gender, physical traits, and aspects of temperament, siblings create differing roles for themselves within the family system. The differing roles in turn lead to disparate ways of currying parental favor." Sulloway is more a Darwinian than a Freudian, but, from the Freudian side, the psychoanalyst Franz Alexander seems to come to the same conclusion when he writes: "Envy and competition are deeply rooted in early family life and are latently present in the adult and influence his relationship to other members of society."

Is the family the seat, then, not only of neurosis, as Freud and the Freudians argue, but also of envy, which, less directly, Sulloway argues? Might envy itself be the source of much neurosis? Intellectually tempting though it may be to agree, many people, consulting their own experience, are likely to find neither of these points registering a very high truth quotient. I happen to be among them. I have known envy, and I am willing to admit to being in many ways quite nutty, if not technically neurotic, but neither envy nor nuttiness began, I believe, in my family. I am pleased to report that I was able to cultivate them outside the house.

Nor does Marxism, which may also be said to be based largely on envy, provide a persuasive argument for the origin of envy. When I say that Marxism is based on envy, I mean that the glorious revolution of the proletariat that it promised was really a promise to put a final end to all the conditions that make for envy. Marxism even posits human nature, and thus human beings, as yearning for equality, a statement that is far from easily proven but upon which Marxism depends for what cogency it might still possess. The great class struggle is about nothing less than the enviable advantages that the upper classes have over the lower—advantages that, even at the cost of bloody revolution, must be eliminated. For this reason Marxism has even been described as a blood cult, with envy its abiding stimulant, fuel, and motive.

Yet it is entirely possible, I suppose, to be a Freudian or a Marxist without being motivated chiefly, or even moderately, by envy. The fact seems to be that there is no predominant human type to which envy attaches itself. Literature shows the envious to take various forms and to hold multifarious traits, from those characters that suffer it in Euripides, Shakespeare, Stendhal, Dickens, Melville, F. Scott Fitzgerald, and beyond. In life, not literature, envy can sneak up on one, and be an intermittent and passing phenomenon; or it can be a dominant, and domineering, element in one's personality. Sometimes it can be coldly rational, sometimes surpassingly goofy. All one can say for certain is that the feeling of envy isn't likely to increase one's capacity for happiness. Quite the reverse.

We all exist on at least three levels: there is the person as he or she appears in public; the person as he or she is known to intimates, which include family and dear friends; and that person, deepest of all, who is only known to him- or herself, where all the aspirations, resentments, fantasies, desires, and much else that is not ready for public knowledge reside. At this last level, where envy also resides, the wattage tends to be kept low, making self-knowledge not all that clear and the law of contradictions carries no authority whatsoever. Here the sub-, if not the un-conscious, often has the whiphand. So one can envy even those things one knows one ought not to have: the extravagant possession, the beautiful if dimwitted lover, the prestige of a job that would otherwise put an end to all one's normal pleasures and destroy one's life. But, then, whoever said that envy made sense?

CHAPTER THREE

Secret Vice

The first recorded case of envy is that of Cain killing his brother Abel. When God found Abel's offering to him of the first of his flock of sheep acceptable and Cain's offering of the fruit of the ground less acceptable, it was too much for Cain, the older brother, to bear. I don't think I give away the plot when I quote Genesis (4:8): "And it came to pass, when they were in the field, that Cain rose up against Abel his brother, and slew him." Those Old Testament characters, like the Old Testament God Himself, were always, as people in the head trades like to say, "acting out." In this instance, Cain was acting out his envy. Not, as he and so many of the envious that have followed have long since learned, a very smart thing to do.

Of the Ten Commandments, the one touching most closely on envy is the sixth: "Thou shalt not covet thy neighbor's house, thou shalt not covet thy neighbor's wife, nor his maidservant, nor his ox, nor his ass, nor anything that is thy neighbor's." To covet means to feel inordinate desire for what belongs to another—in a word, to envy it. The act of coveting, as the author of the Commandments, a close student of the human heart, well knew, is at the center of envy. My neighbor, my friend, even my brother has something I do not: anything ranging from acceptance in the eyes of God to a stronger ox than my own down to things barely measurable. This, for the envious, is intolerable.

Why does he have it and not I? That is the chief, perhaps the only, question, for the envious, who have a deeper, if only because more solipsistic, sense of injustice than others. They also have a restless competitiveness, which will not cease nagging away at them until they feel themselves clearly established as first among unequals. They feel a fundamental unfairness, lashed up with an abiding sense of grudgingness, in the disposition of any good in which they are not the most favored recipients. Why should the next fellow have the more capacious house, beautiful wife, better job, sweeter life than I? The answer is clear: he, the son of a bitch, should not.

Although those of us who have felt genuine envy will not require any elaborate explanation of what is distinctive about the feeling, permit me to attempt a brief psychological description for those perhaps too gentle readers who have been able to elude the feeling. You see something, want it, feel it only sensible and right that it belong to you and not the person who has it. Once the injustice of the other person having it is established—this doesn't usually take too long—his unworthiness must be emphasized, at least in your own mind. Your own greater worthiness goes quite without saying. His loathsomeness doesn't; it may be said over and over, to yourself. Whatever the object of inordinate desire—an item of art or luxury, the friendship or love of another person, the prestige that goes with a position or place or prize in life—the world begins to seem out of joint, so long as he has it and you do not. The quality of your feeling in connection with it becomes obsessional. You find yourself thinking about it more than you know you ought, find it difficult to think of other things. (An obsession, after all, is something that one returns to again and again—can't, really, leave alone.)

Balance and perspective on the object of one's envy are soon enough lost. If you are clever and retain some self-control, you will know not to speak about anything to do with the subject. If you are less clever and out of control, you will speak too often about it, thus tipping your mitt about your (somewhat) deranged feeling. But either way, roiling within, or exposed without, envy doesn't tend to remind you of the dignity of humankind, let alone of your own dignity. If envy leads you to any fresh self-knowledge, your opinion of yourself is likely to suffer because of it.

The object of envy, it needs to be emphasized, has to know certain bounds. One of the most popular people in the city of Chicago for many years was the Chicago Bears running back, the late Walter Payton. A very great athlete, he won all the emoluments to which his ability on the field entitled him: those true desires of Freud's sublimationally dreaming artist, fame, money, power, and the love of beautiful women. (He also happens to have been, from all accounts, a gent, as befits a man with the nickname of Sweetness.) My envying Walter Payton anything is absurd. I don't have the imagination to sustain such envy, and if I did envy Walter Payton, feeling that what he had ought really to have been mine, I should have to be judged, rightly I think, insane.

I learn, from a newspaper item, that Katie Couric, the morning talk show person, is to get more than $15 million a year to sign her *Today Show* contract with NBC. Should I be envious of this salary? No, because to earn that much money on television one probably has to have a mind not very different from Ms. Couric's, and having it wouldn't be worth $30 million a year.

But am I insane to envy a not very good writer who wins a MacArthur Fellowship, which pays him roughly half-a-million dollars for doing absolutely nothing more than remaining his mediocre self?

Would I be wrong to envy a university teacher who earns twice what I do while teaching—and teaching, from all reports, rather badly—half as much?

Where does a sense of the world's injustice end and envy begin? Rather than spot envy in oneself, it seems so much more convenient instead to lay one's envious feelings off on one's good taste, keen critical sense, scrupulous judgment. "The light of envy, the light of loathing, the light of pride," remarks Paul Valéry's Monsieur Teste, " . . . Who does not have his sensitive points? His natural wounds, his wise, subtle, and fundamental sufferings, his true flesh all the more sensitive for being deep?" Envy being too ugly a feeling to admit to the world, the care one takes to camouflage it usually ends in disguising it from oneself.

Degrees of envy exist, of course, some mild, some strong, some cool, others hot. Where envy turns ugly is when it turns pure: when, that is, one doesn't even require any advantage for oneself but is perfectly content to make sure that the next person derives no advantage. A joke that nicely illustrates the point tells of an Englishwoman, a Frenchman, and a Russian, who are each given a single wish by one of those genies whose almost relentless habit it is to pop out of bottles. The Englishwoman says that a friend of hers has a charming cottage in the Cotswolds, and that she would like a similar cottage, with the addition of two extra bedrooms and a second bath and a brook running in front of it.

The Frenchman says that his best friend has a beautiful blonde mistress, and he would like such a mistress himself, but a redhead instead of a blonde and with longer legs and a bit more in the way of culture and *chic*. The Russian, when asked what he would like, tells of a neighbor who has a cow that gives a vast quantity of the richest milk, which yields the heaviest cream and the purest butter. "I vant dat cow," the Russian tells the genie, "dead."

CHAPTER FOUR

Is Beauty Friendless?

Do men or women feel envy more strongly? This is a question dangerously close to that which Hera and Zeus asked Tiresias, the legendary seer who had inhabited the body of both a man and a woman, about who enjoys sex more, men or women. When the poor fellow reported that women enjoyed sex more, Hera, who took these things hard, put out his eyes.

The question of who feels envy more strongly also happens to be a question without an answer, at least by any contemporary social-scientific standard. Yet one senses that, for the most part, men and women have taken up different objects about which to be envious. My guess—now there is a highly social-scientific word—is that men do more envying in the purely sexual realm.

"Do I detect a new resentment?"

Men tend to be greatly put off—in this context, "envious" is the more precise word—by what is usually called "an offensively good-looking man." What offends, of course, is not his looks, but what he can get with them—women. Woman chasing is perhaps the oldest male sport, and to be thought too well equipped for it is automatically to court envy.

But, then, it may well be that much of male envy generally is linked to sexual success or the prospects of such success. David

Reisman, as far back as the 1950s, in his book *The Lonely Crowd*, notes that most modern men seem to be able to live with other men having grander possessions, but the thought of someone else having a more interesting sex life is, somehow, intolerable. ("The other-directed person has no defense against his own envy . . . he does not want to miss . . . the qualities of experience he tells himself the others are having.") One of the things that makes this seem cogent if not altogether convincing is that so much envy appears to be along what I think of as same-sex lines. When envy crops up, or so it seems to me, only rarely does it do so on the part of a man envying a woman. In corporations, it may be that several male vice presidents are filled with envy for the company's female CEO. But for the most part—and for complex reasons—men, even highly envious men, tend not to envy women their money, beautiful objects, or power in the world. They envy instead other men who are able to attract the attention of women.

When women envy men, the envy seems to be of a more general nature. I once sat at lunch with a woman writer who, in bemoaning her loneliness, told me that she couldn't help thinking how different her condition would be if she were a male writer, a man who, like her, was in her early fifties and had published three books. "I'd have a full social life, with lots of interested young women," she said. "But as a woman of 54, despite my literary accomplishments, I'm not considered all that attractive, eligible, sexy. It would be completely different if I were a man." I think she was probably right.

The modern feminist movement can, I believe, be said to have been built on an impersonal, generalized envy. Women wanted what men seemed to have: freedom of choice in career, in mates, in living with the same irresponsibility (in every field of endeavor) as men. Most women would say, I suspect, that not envy but a strong sense of injustice powered the feminist movement. They would not be wrong, but I would only add that envy and a sense of injustice are not always that easily distinguished, let alone extricated, one from the other.

One can imagine a woman, or a number of women, envious of a too beautiful woman capturing all the interest of the men in the room. (Schopenhauer said that a truly beautiful woman will have no genuine women friends.) One can imagine a woman envious of another woman who appears to have had better luck in the lottery of life. One can, most easily of all, imagine a woman envious of the accomplishments of the children of a friend that rise above those of her own children.

The envy of women strikes me as usually personal and particular, as envy ought to be, while that of men can often be wilder and zanier, more often built on fantasy and overestimation of the self. Possibly this is owing to men's having had more freedom, freedom that, as like as not, they choose not to put to use. A friend of mine recently asked me if I knew many woman chasers. I allowed as how I knew a few. "You know," he said, "they almost never have any regrets, except maybe that they didn't chase even more women." I could hear the faint stirrings of envy in my friend's voice. I could have counseled him that a great deal of sexual variety isn't a true replacement for real love; I tell myself that it isn't; in fact, I know that it isn't. But I am also a man and cannot help wondering why I couldn't have had both, immense variety and genuine love in inexhaustible supply.

The envy of men is more far-flung than that of women. For men everything seems possible, not least the highly improbable. Men can envy athletes when they themselves have little coordination and less physical courage; men of great wealth even though they themselves have neither business acumen nor much in the way of ambition; artists when they themselves have no craft or artistic skill whatsoever.

Not long ago I was watching, on PBS, a taped version of Simon and Garfunkle's Concert in Central Park. Although I write no songs, have a poor singing voice, and play no instrument, none of this stopped me from mocking Paul Simon's wretched hairpiece or the thinness of his sensitive little songs, when what I was really thinking was: Why does this guy command the attention of hundreds of thousands of New Yorkers half high on pot and why isn't the same adoration accorded me? Utterly daft, of course, but there it is.

Might it be that men do not for the most part envy women because they view women as one of life's prizes? (A CEO, in the business section of the *New York Times*, explained to his stockholders that their company's profits were partly down because too much money had been spent the previous year on wine, women, and song; and he promised that in the current year management, under his leadership, would cut down drastically on song.) Women do not look upon men in anything like the same way. But now that their liberation has allowed them entry in the great sweepstakes of the world's prizes, I wonder if they won't fall victim to all the other realms of envy—small and large, realistic and goofy—to which men have been prey. If they do—and I suspect they will—then one can only welcome them to the carnival with its carousel of desires that seem never to relent, desires that stir competitive feelings, fantastical hopes, infuriating disappointments. Welcome, ladies, to the world of the envious.

The Glittering Prizes

What has the world designated as enviable? At a certain level of generality, wealth, beauty, power, talent and skill, knowledge and wisdom, and extraordinary good luck come close to completing the list. (I'd add youth, more about which presently.) Some of these items are gifts received at birth; some are acquired at the expense of great effort. In the best of all worlds, one would be rich, beautiful, powerful, laden with talent, wise and learned, and (given the foregoing) obviously hugely fortunate. In the actual world, one is considered fairly lucky if in possession of any one of these items.

If one does have one or more than one of these enviable qualities, the chances are great that it is not that which one most wanted. I have never known a beautiful woman, for example,

"I say we don't trust anyone under thirty with a billion dollars."

who didn't feel her beauty decisively flawed by some (usually) minuscule portion of her physique that she can't bear. ("Look at my ankles, for God's sake!") Unless this is envy speaking, most immensely handsome men turn out to be rather lunkheaded; perhaps their handsomeness has made it easier for them not to have to work overlong at cultivating their intelligence. The rich want to be beautiful or wish themselves wise; and the wise, if they really are wise, know that the wisdom begins with the acknowledgement that one knows nothing, so, really, what the hell good is that.

F. Scott Fitzgerald said: "I didn't have the top two things, great animal magnetism or money. I had the second two things, though, good looks and intelligence." I don't believe Fitzgerald was an envious man—his false friend Ernest Hemingway, I believe, was deeply envious—but, as a fantast of sorts, Fitzgerald did know a vast deal about yearning. My guess is that, had he the money, he wouldn't have minded throwing those Long Island parties of Jay Gatsby's; and there is no doubt he would have loved having those delightful shirts. He may even have wanted to marry a woman like Daisy Buchanan, formerly of Lake Forest, Illinois, a Daisy in a more kind-hearted version, of course. But as an artist, F. Scott Fitzgerald could, through the alchemy of art, transform his envy into yearning and then—*prestidigitato*—into art.

The rest of us are left to deal with our envy in less magical ways. Fortunately, for most of us our envy is of small things and of brief duration. I see the grace and strength of a male ballet dancer and wish I could command something similar on my own. I read a book studded with brilliant insights set out in unblemished prose and wish I had had the thoughtfulness and craft to have written it myself. I go to lunch with three friends and when the main courses arrive, I see that I have ordered quite the poorest dish of the four of us at the table and, looking at theirs, I feel a stab of disappointment accompanied by what I call "entrée envy." (*Futterneid* is the German word for food envy generally.) But these are all fleeting feelings, as close to wistfulness as they are to true envy.

Helmut Schoeck in his book on envy makes the point that real envy is reserved not for the great or the greatly gifted, but for those whose situation seems only slightly better than ours. "Overwhelming and astounding inequality," he writes, "especially when it has an element of the unattainable, arouses far less envy than minimal inequality, which inevitably causes the envious to think: 'I might have been in his place.'"

Something to it, I believe. Impossible to envy Bill Gates—not a hugely attractive human being in any case—but it can be irritating to learn that someone doing the same work you do is paid $10,000 a year more. Easy, too, to envy the lucky: people who, inexplicably, just happen to have been in the right place at the right time, or been put on to a good thing, or seem to have the mysterious touch that makes money, attracts love, puts them in the perpetually advantageous position.

Envy runs high in the world of art and intellect. Unpopular authors often envy popular ones, unless the popularity of the latter is so large and vulgar that the former can pick up the slack of envy through the palliative of snobbery and write off their success as owing to their inherent vulgarity. Intense competitiveness among peers can induce envy: rarely, in my observation, do the top three or four people in any line of intellectual endeavor have kind words to say about the others. Envy usually kicks in when one appears to jump slightly ahead of the pack. Some atmospheres are more envy-charged than others; the novelist and screenwriter Frederick Raphael speaks of "the envy and glitter of London life." Life among the artists, writers, and intellectuals of New York does not seem to me greatly dissimilar. How little it takes to make one academic sick with envy over the pathetically small advantages won by another: the better office, the slightly lighter teaching load, the fickle admiration of students. For years in universities, if a scholar wrote well and commanded a wider than merely scholarly audience because of the accessibility of his prose, he was put down as a "popularizer." Pure envy talking, of course.

My late and dear mother, who had a taste for glitz, used to drive rather flashy Cadillacs. Once, in a traffic jam at O'Hare airport, I suggested to her that she put out her arm in the hope that someone would give her a break by allowing her to get into the stream of moving traffic in the next lane. "Not likely to happen," she said, looking at me as the simple naïf I am. "With this car, people assume that you have already had your break."

Studies such as Robert H. Frank's *Luxury Fever* have shown that people would agree to make less total money so long as they make more than their neighbors: that is, they would rather earn, say, $85,000 a year where no one else is making more than $75,000 instead of $100,000 where everyone else is making $125,000. H. L. Mencken, who took especial delight in the frailties and the pretensions of the democratic spirit, once defined contentment in America as making $10 a month more than your brother-in-law.

A recent fortune cookie of mine reads, "It is better to be envied than to be pitied." But it is not clear that everyone would agree. "The best condition in life," notes Josh Billings, "is not to be so rich as to be envied, nor so poor as to be damned." Others would prefer the riches and be willing to let them bring on the envy. A person competitive and rivalrous by nature might even prefer being envied—might not find life quite worthwhile without encouraging a faint or possibly strong feeling of hopelessness in his friends, family, and everyone else around him.

Most simple tribes lived in a terror of being envied; they worried about the reactions of fellow tribesmen, of neighboring tribes, but above all they worried about the wrath of the gods at their good fortune. Helmut Schoeck writes: "Nearly all superstition can be found to derive its dynamic from this particular anxiety about envy, and may be interpreted as a system of ritual environmental control directed against envy." Some of this continues into our own day. Catholics cross themselves. *Kein ayin hora*, the Jews of a certain generation used to say, meaning, may the evil eye not confound my good luck. Knock wood, more secular-minded people say, when hoping their good fortune will continue. I myself frequently knock wood, after saying *kein ayin hora*. What can it hurt, right?

When I first set out to write about envy, a magazine editor to whom I mentioned it asked me if I realized I was of course myself highly enviable. Truth to tell, I'd thought of myself as lucky but scarcely enviable. When I asked how so, she replied that my work was in demand at most serious magazines; that I made a decent living doing the thing I loved best; that I received lots of recognition and praise; and that, because of all this, mine seemed one of those charmed lives. Whatever there may or may not be to it, I have to assert that I do not feel particularly enviable. Certainly nowhere near in the way of Goethe, of whom Max Scheler, author of *Ressentiment*, writes, that he, Goethe, knew that "his great and rich existence . . . his very appearance, was bound to make the poison flow."

I do not feel enviable so much as I feel lucky: lucky to have found my *métier*, and found it fairly early in life and been allowed to practice it without great obstacles having been put in my way; having over the years found, too, my just audience; having, finally, been left time to do my work in an atmosphere without constraint of any kind. I don't find any of this very enviable, but just damned, immeasurably, wonderfully lucky.

But has my sustained good luck—knock wood and *kein ayin hora*—now elevated me to the ranks of the enviable? I find it difficult to believe so. Yet I note that I have become more and more secretive about good things that, professionally, come my way. I like to think that bragging has never been my way, but now, having been warned that I may be enviable, not bragging because of the concern about incurring envy has entered my consciousness. So if you ask me how well my last book did, or what fee I received for a magazine article or a talk, expect me not to look you quite in the eye and to be lied to in a downward direction.

CHAPTER SIX

The Young,
God Damn Them

Among those things the world has judged enviable, perhaps only one comes close to garnering near universal agreement: youth. Even the most generous-hearted cannot, at times, help envying the young, if for nothing more complicated than the undeniable fact that the most important cards of life, the years, are stacked in their favor. I wouldn't want to be young again, one says, and yet to say it is probably to suggest, perhaps unbeknownst to oneself, one's fatigue with life.

Obviously the young do not feel envious of youth—they find other things to envy: wealth, position, experience, power—but

"Your metabolism is the envy of everyone at this party."

nearly everyone else who feels his or her own youth beginning to depart or entirely gone cannot look upon the glowing young, *le jeunesse dorée*, without an accompanying sigh of yearning that easily enough melds into envy. Much of this envy of the young is of a general and harmless kind, but sometimes it can turn particular and quite poisonous.

The young have health, energy, solid well-formed flesh, and, usually, very little notion that life has a finish line. Pointless, it seems, to remind them that, when last calculated, the mortality rate remains at 100 percent. Many years ago, when I was the director of the Anti-Poverty Program in Little Rock, Arkansas, a program was proposed called "Foster Grandparents," which would allow the elderly poor to make money by watching over children when the children's parents went to work. The problem turned out to be that the old were not always—were not even usually—all that enamored of the very young. As often as not, they even rather disliked these small creatures who would roam the earth for so long after they, the elderly, were under it. The program, not allowing for the envy of the young by the old, never really worked out.

One sometimes wonders if the so-called conflict of generations, refreshed and renewed every 20 or so years, isn't in good part not so much a conflict as a supercharged emotional relationship sparked and fueled on the part of the older generations by envy. Frequently it's envy tinged with regret. One sees beautiful young people and, remembering one's own youth, feels sorrow at not having made more of it. This sorrowful regret, with a twist of anger added, easily turns into envy. The poet Dick Allen writes:

> The pretty young bring to the coarsely old
> *Rechaffé* dishes, but the sauce is cold.

Envy of the young, then, seems bound up with regret and yearning. When it comes to regret and yearning, the poet par excellence is Philip Larkin. Self-described as looking like "a bald salmon," Larkin wore glasses, was overweight, and was a fairly serious boozer. He seemed to have had the dubious gift of perpetual middle age, and couldn't take his eye off his own mortality. (He died at 63.) Although not without lady friends, he often made himself sound the very model of the repressed, deprived man. His poems are rife with longing, much of it openly sexual longing, and the strong sense of having always, somehow, managed to miss the boat. One of his most famous poems begins:

> Sexual intercourse began
> In nineteen sixty-three
> (Which was rather late for me)—
> Between the end of the *Chatterley* ban
> And the Beatles' first LP.

It gets worse. Suddenly the quarrelling and bargaining about sex that was standard practice in his own youth was over, Larkin's poem declares, and:

> Everyone felt the same
> And every life became

A brilliant breaking of the bank
A quite unlosable game.

Except, of course, for Philip Larkin. In the poem "High Windows" he notes seeing a couple of kids and imagines they are fornicating away like wildebeests, living in a paradise never opened, and now permanently closed off, to him. This paradise that

Everyone old has dreamed of all their lives
Bonds and gestures pushed to one side
Like an outdated combine harvester,
And everyone young going down the long slide
To happiness, endlessly.

Everyone, once again, except for Larkin.

Imagine, please, introducing Philip Larkin to an English movie actor named Paul Bettany, whom I read about in a brief piece in the May 2002 issue of *Esquire* under the rubric "Envy This Man." The journalist writing the piece, who deserves to be nameless for his happy witlessness, though Paul Bettany's exact contemporary, allows that the actor is four inches taller than he, "squarer of jaw, and way more British." Bettany is allowed a few quick quotations, all of which make reference to the private parts, and ends by recounting an anecdote about a woman who picks him up at a bar and threatens to take him home to give him a very strenuous sexual workout. Philip, Paul—Paul, Phil.

I don't happen to envy Paul Bettany in the least. I shouldn't want to inhabit his body if his mind came with it, which, somehow, I have the strong feeling it would. No, what I believe one envies in the young is, in part, what one takes to be the excellence of their physiology—organs and entrails, parts and appendages, all in smooth working order—and, accompanying this, their ability to live the appetitive life without the sometimes small but always nagging punishments that are inflicted when attempted by the older.

But more than this envy of a sounder physical system, the old—even the merely older—envy the young their chance still to write an impressive record on the many days of life remaining to them. Rare is the man or woman who doesn't yearn for a second draft on much of his or her life: all the things they would have done differently, the roads not taken, the opportunities blown, muffed, not even dimly glimpsed when they first arose. The young, damn them, still have a shot at it all, while one's own gunpowder has been spent firing at delectable animals— pheasants long disappeared into the brush—that, it turns out, may never really have been there.

Youth, it has almost too famously been said, is wasted on the young. And of course it is. If the young had the experience of the aged, they probably wouldn't have the pleasure in their youth-fulness that being inexperienced brings. The cruel deal seems to be this: one is permitted all the physical gifts so long as one doesn't really know how to husband them; and one learns how to husband them only when these gifts have departed. The comedy of all comedies is herein played. God, we must once more conclude, loves a joke.

But the best play of all takes place where all this rivalrousness among generations is eliminated and—apologies for sounding the Hallmark-card note here—love conquers all. In her autobi-ography, the writer Iris Origo, author of books on Byron and Leopardi, writes about her Irish grandfather, Lord Desart, in the most endearingly appreciative way, and from the two letters from him that I am about to quote you will soon enough discover why.

After a long separation from his still young granddaughter Iris, Lord Desart writes: "From a purely personal standpoint, I think I feel most the long severance from Mummy and you. She perhaps will be much the same when we meet again, but you are at a time when every day, month and year changes your outlook and standards. . . . You will be a different Iris when we meet, and I shall have to begin knowing you again. You may no longer think of me as an amiable elderly relation, but an obsolete old buffer out of touch with your interests and sympathies. But believe me, I shall never be that."

And then, when Iris grows older, her grandfather writes: "I shall have lost the child I loved so well, but perhaps find the young woman I shall love even better. Our outlooks may be different, but love is the most real thing in life, and there are certain elemental things to which young and old are equally applicable. You have too much sense of humor to allow yourself, with the different ideals of another generation, to be contemptuous of what older people think and do. It is the intolerance of the young and the want of sympathy of the old that produces much unnecessary unhappiness in family life, and I trust we may avoid it."

And they did, always and forever, and neither envy nor any other dark feeling was ever permitted to touch the lovely relationship between two.

CHAPTER SEVEN

Knavery's Plain Face

Distinctions among the envious and envying need to be made. Some of us know envy only fleetingly. Damn, should have ordered the grilled salmon, as she did. Some of us, being naturally competitive and rivalrous, have an envious tendency if not full-blown nature. Why should he get all the attention? And some people are pathologically envious. Envy is of the air they breathe, conditioning their outlook, motivations, point of view—it's a way of life. Demographically, the largest population of the envious are of course those who know it fleetingly, followed by those for whom envy is a tendency. As for the pathologically envious, I cannot say that I have ever met such a person—except in literature.

Even here the number of the envious is fewer than that of the jealous. The jealous husband or wife, the jealous lover generally, is a fairly stock figure in novels and plays. But envy, being a more devious condition than jealousy, does not reveal itself so readily. If the novel exists that is narrated by a man or women driven chiefly by envy, I do not know it. Great literary skill would be required to write it and not make the envious narrator utterly loathsome.

Consider such a character (who does not narrate), the odious Uriah Heep, from Dickens's *David Copperfield*. His pathetic pretense of humility—he's always so "umble"—turns out in the end to be a cover for his deep social envy of his employers, the Wickfields, whose daughter he hopes to force into a marriage. But he most deeply envies David Copperfield, who has climbed higher with even less behind him than has Heep.

" 'You are a precious set of people, ain't you,' said Heep in the same low voice, and breaking out into a clammy heat, which he wiped from his forehead, with his long lean hand, 'to buy over my clerk, who is the very scum of society,—as you yourself were, Copperfield, before anyone had any charity on you—to defame me with his lies.' "

David Copperfield, a page or so later in the novel, remarks: "Though I had long known that his [Uriah Heep's] servility was false, I had no adequate conception of the extent of his hypocrisy, until I now saw him with his mask off. The suddenness with which he dropped it, when he perceived that it was useless to him; the malice, insolence, and hatred he revealed; the leer with which he exulted, even at this moment, in the evil he had done—all this time being desperate too, and at his wits' end for the means of getting the better of us—though perfectly consistent with the experience I had of him, at first took even me by surprise, who had known him so long, and disliked him so heartily."

The moral of the story, for students of envy, is that one never knows how deep it runs, for it can be—like Uriah Heep's hypocrisy, malice, hatred, and insolence—bottomless. "'Tis here, but yet confused Knavery's plain face is never seen till used."

That line belongs to Iago, in Act II, Scene 1 of *Othello*, and one can only say that it takes one to know one. By this criterion, Iago knows better than anyone else. In the realm of envy, he is surely the supreme creation, the envier of all enviers—and a man who acts on his envy, to the bloody end of nearly everyone else in the play that, in my view, he steals: *Iago*, it ought to have been called, not *Othello*. The play is often thought the great work on jealousy—which, as Iago warns Othello, is "the green eyed monster which doth mock/the meat it feeds on"—and it is that, but it is envy that calls the tune and gets things humming: setting everything in action, moving the characters about as if they were so many pieces of furniture, forging and forcing the denouement.

As with all Shakespeare's plays, there is a great swamp, a big muddy, of criticism instructing one how to read *Othello*, and providing guidance on the character of Iago. I think he is better understood not as a character of pure evil—though, God knows, he is evil enough—but one behind whose evil lurks envy. He envies Cassio his having been appointed ahead of him as Othello's lieutenant; he may envy Othello an earlier dalliance with his, Iago's, wife Emilia; but perhaps above all he envies Othello the grandeur of his character, the quality he has of operating on the large scale. As Iago's evil is conditioned by envy, so is his hatred fed by it all the way through the play. Such are the multifarious and mysterious forms that envy may take; it can almost be disinterested, attaching itself to things that do not, in the strict sense, stand it in its way, as Cassio, in Shakespeare's play, stands in the way of Iago.

Consider *Billy Budd, Sailor,* the greatest story in Western literature with pure envy at its center. Early in the story, Herman Melville reminds us that Satan himself suffered from envy, and most of his actions proceeded therefrom. "In this particular," he writes, his innocent and handsome sailor Billy Budd "was a striking instance that the arch interferer, the envious marplot of Eden, still has more or less to do with every human consignment to this planet Earth. In every case, one way or another, he is sure to slip in his little card, as much as to remind us—I too have a hand here."

Billy Budd, Sailor is the story of a good man brought down by a bad man for no other reason than that the latter hates the former's good looks and the purity of his innocent large heartedness. From first sight, John Claggart, master-at-arms of the HMA *Bellepoint*, feels the gall of envy at the sight of "the welkin-eyed" Billy, and to the gall of his envy, Melville reports, he adds the vitriol of contempt.

Melville claims that he shall essay a portrait of John Claggart, "but never hit it." Claggart is a carrier of what Melville calls "Natural Depravity," which he limns as of a kind to be found not in jails but in civilization, folded in "the mantle of respectability," never "mercenary or avaricious," nor "sordid or sensual," deeply irrational under the guise of a reasoned life. Those who have this natural depravity, writes Melville, "are madmen, and of the most dangerous sort, for their lunacy is not continuous, but occasional, evoked by some special object; it is protectively secretive, which is as much to say it is self-contained, so that when, moreover, most active it is to the average mind not distinguishable from sanity, and for the reason above suggested: that whatever its aims may be—and the aim is never declared—the method and the outward proceeding are always perfectly rational."

As the story moves to its inexorably tragic close, Melville, in very few strokes, shows the monomania behind Claggart's envy of Billy Budd. Melville turns out to be a perceptive anatomist of envy. Descanting upon the subject in a slightly digressive mode in the middle of his story, he tells us that, "though many an arraigned mortal has in hopes of mitigated penalty pleaded guilty to horrible actions, did ever anybody seriously confess to envy?" He adds: "And not only does everybody disown it, but the better sort are inclined to incredulity when it is in earnest imputed to an intelligent man. But since its lodgment is in the heart not the brain, no degree of intellect supplies a guarantee against it."

Claggart's envious hatred of Billy causes him to bear false witness against him. When confronted by his accuser, the pure Billy, afflicted by his stutter, is unable to answer and so reacts—instinctively, fatally—with a single blow that drops John Claggart to his death. The blow is doubly fatal, for Billy Budd, though innocent in heart, must be punished by hanging for what he has done. Melville's final word on these events is given to Captain Vere, Starry Vere as this meditative man is known, who claims that the events that have taken place are a mystery, "but to use a scriptural phrase, it is a mystery of iniquity, a matter for psychologic theologians to discuss." The real mystery, in other words, is who put the envy in John Claggart's heart.

Who puts envy in anyone's heart? More than a hundred years since Melville wrote his story, we still don't know, are still awaiting that brilliant visionary psychologic theologian to tell us.

CHAPTER EIGHT

Under Capitalism Man Envies Man; Under Socialism, Vice Versa

Greed is said to be the sin of capitalist societies, envy that of socialist ones. There is something—quite a lot, actually—to it. Putting the best possible face on things, some say that greed is little more than emulative envy. Capitalism allows one the liberty to be as rich as—or, better, richer than—everyone else. Socialism, flying under the flag of equality, seeks a society in which no one has anything more than anyone else: "From each according to his abilities, to each according to his needs," to quote a sentence that once had a lot more resonance in the world than it does today.

The doctrine of Marxism is many things, but one among them is a plan of revenge for the envious. How else can one view Karl Marx's central idea, the perpetual class struggle, ending in the defeat and eradication of the aristocracy, the rentier class, the bourgeois, everyone, really, but the working class, which will arise at last in the form of the glorious dictatorship of the proletariat? "It is only in Marxism, the abstract and glorified concept of the proletariat, the disinherited, and exploited," writes Helmut Schoeck, "that a position of implacable envy is fully legitimized." In certain minds, Marxism can be seen as less a body of economic theory than as an act of collective vengeance: soak the rich, is its rally cry, in their own blood, is implied.

Envy could be construed as injustice brought down to the personal level. Why him and not me? The fundamental question of the envious is at bottom a question about the injustice of the way the world has things arranged. One of the evils socialism was to eliminate, along with injustice, was envy itself. With everyone being equal, nothing would be left to envy. The problem, as the actual experience of revolutionary socialism revealed, was that some would be more equal than others, which put them in a position to crush the rest, which they, once established as first among equals, seem to have had a propensity to do, and, as history has shown, often—as in the Soviet Union and Mao's China—in appallingly large numbers.

Envy becomes political when it becomes generalized. It becomes generalized when a large, or at least ample, section of society feels, as John Rawls puts it in his *Theory of Justice*, an unfairness on the part of those "more favored for the kinds of goods they possess and not for the particular objects they possess. The upper classes are envied for their greater wealth and opportunity; those who envy them want similar advantages for themselves." Particular envy is more individual, more personal, more single-mindedly covetous, and tends to blame the gods and not any social system for its being.

In Rawls's words, "We may think of envy as the propensity to view with hostility the greater good of others even though their being more fortunate than we does not detract from our advantages." So viewed, "Envy is collectively disadvantageous; the individual who envies another is prepared to do things that make them both worse off, if only the discrepancy between them is sufficiently reduced." One sees this on those occasions when class warfare really is roaring. During the late 1970s and early '80s, when the British trade unions seemed to have a stranglehold on British industry, an English friend of mine, himself born into the working class, reported to me that, when told that their aggressive behavior threatened to sink the economy of the country, British labor unionists were likely to reply: "That's O.K. here, mate, so long as those upper-class bastards go down with us." There speaks envy in its most aggressive political form.

In John Rawls's opinion, a well-ordered society will do much "to mitigate if not prevent" the conditions that make for envy. Through its institutions, among them those allowing truly evenhanded justice and proximate equality of opportunity, it can take the sting out of serious disparities of possessions among its citizens. He remarks, too, that "the plurality of voluntary associations [churches, clubs, unions, and other groupings] in a well-ordered society, each with its own secure internal life, tends to reduce the visibility, or at least the painful visibility, of variations in men's prospects." All this presumes that the advantaged do not make an ostentatious display of their advantages "calculated to demean the condition of those who have less"—not, in a world more and more enthralled by advertising, an easy thing to guarantee. Envy, as John Rawls well recognized, presents a problem for any society that likes to think of itself as just, and one neither rightly gainsaid nor easily guarded against.

A problem on a larger scale is that presented by envy on the international scene. Many—one is inclined to write "most"—

wars have been fought because of one nation's envy of another's territory and all the riches that derive from it, or out of jealously guarded riches that another nation feels are endangered by those less rich who are therefore likely to be envious of their superior position. The politics of balancing power have been employed to prevent these jungle-like conditions and impulses to rule supreme, sometimes with more success than at others.

Then there is the strong envy that the people in one nation feel for those in another, whom they feel have it too easy. When one sees the forms this can take, it is difficult not to feel that much anti-Americanism has envy at its heart. "The emotional leitmotifs of anti-Americanism," writes Timothy Garton Ash, in an essay titled "Anti-Europeanism in America," "are resentment mingled with envy." Envy of this kind flared up in an ugly way after the 11 September 2001 terrorist attack on the World Trade Center in New York. Although many anti-American intellectuals in other countries claimed that the attack came as a direct result of United States foreign policy, one sniffed something more personally rancorous behind these claims. Writing in such magazines as *The London Review of Books* and *Granta*, European and other non-American intellectuals weighed in with the notion that America somehow deserved what had happened, implying that, with any justice at all, more of the same kind would be coming its way, and rightly so.

Some of this anti-Americanism was of the standard brand. The playwright Harold Pinter hits the note nicely when he calls America "arrogant, indifferent [to human suffering, one assumes], contemptuous of International law," all of which has brought about "a profound revulsion and disgust with the manifestations of American power and global capitalism."

Standard stuff, as I say, but what was other than standard was the piercing note of envy, struck, for example, in the magazine *Granta,* by the Turkish novelist Orhan Pamuk, whose first memory of America was of a little American boy, living in his building in Istanbul, who had marbles of a much higher quality than any Turkish marbles and used to drop them from the balcony on Pamuk and his friends on the street below: a metaphor for the lofty contempt that came with American opulence. In the same magazine, Ramachandra Guha, an Indian writer, wrote that "historically, anti-Americanism in India was shaped by an aesthetic distaste for America's greatest gift—the making of money." Ariel Dorfman, an American who has become a Chilean citizen, tells of watching an annoying American child fall into a pool and begin to drown, while he himself felt "a pang of indifference" at the sight—"that it was none of my business, that in some perverse sense the kid had it coming to him." Happily to report, Dorfman did scoop the child out of the water, and he later remarks on his own ultimately murderous emotion, but one has to wonder where such hatred derives if not from a very deep envy.

"The searing heart-burn of envy," says a character in a novella titled *Envy* (1927), written and set in the Soviet Union by Y. Olesha. "Envy causes a choking feeling in the throat, squeezes the eyes out of their sockets." The characters in this novel are living in a purely socialist, nightmarishly bureaucratized society, and those whose sensitivity has not yet been rooted out of them, know that their lives have been horribly stunted. "I was sorry for him," the narrator of the story says of his father. "He could no longer be handsome or famous, he was a finished product, he could never be anything." Nor can anyone else in this novel, including the narrator, except the arid Soviet model of a bureaucrat working for the glory of the state. One of the main figures in the story, a figure of great prestige, is at work designing the perfect sausage.

"Only not for us," says the apparently (but not really) mad character Ivan Babichev to his daughter, "all that is left for us is envy and more envy. . . . " Envy and indifference: "I'd go as far as to say that indifference is the finest attribute of the human mind," this same Ivan Babichev remarks. "Let's cultivate indifference." The moral of Olesha's dark little story seems to be that all that remains to those trapped in a putatively envy-free society is envy for those who are able to live outside it. And of course no society was more envy-ridden than the late (and not in the least lamented) Soviet Union, where turning in one's neighbors for their perceived advantages allowed envy to become a way of life and a way to get a leg up.

No Utopia yet invented, no matter how brutal it has been willing to be in the name of its own idealism, has been able to root out envy.

CHAPTER NINE

Our Good Friends, the Jews

Are Jews enviable? One wouldn't, straightaway, have thought so. For much of their history, the Jews have been officially judged, in the various countries in which during their long Diaspora they have shored up, less as enviable than as execrable. Anti-Semitism was for too many centuries a hatred that, only until recently, did indeed dare to speak, even shout, its name. Might it be that behind this long hatred lay envy in one of the most hideous forms it has ever taken?

When one contemplates the often-impressive financial and occupational success of Jews in the modern world, one's social radar senses envy as a frequent reaction to it. Consider these rough statistics from the Vienna of 1936, a city that was 90 percent Catholic and 9 percent Jewish: Jews accounted for 60 percent of the city's lawyers, more than half its physicians, more than 90 percent of its advertising executives, and 123 of its 174 newspaper editors. And this is not to mention the prominent places Jews held in banking, retailing, and intellectual and artistic life. The numbers four or five years earlier for Berlin are said to have been roughly similar.

One has of course to ask if this astonishing success of mostly assimilated Jews doesn't have a direct connection with the beastly way the Germans and Austrians treated their Jewish countrymen when the Nazis came to power. Earlier antagonists of the Jews— barbaric Russian pogromists, coarse Polish peasants, vengeance-seeking Arabs—thought little of killing Jews in brutish ways. But the Nazis, though they went in for a vaster scale of Jew-killing than any others, seemed to need to humiliate their victims first, at least in Germany and Austria, where they had Jewish women cleaning floors, had Jewish physicians scrubbing the cobblestone streets of Vienna with toothbrushes as Nazi youth urinated on them, and forced elderly Jews to do hundreds of deep knee bends until they fainted or sometimes died. All this suggests a vicious evening of the score that has the ugly imprint of envy on the loose all over it. The Jews in Germany and Austria had succeeded not only beyond their numbers but also, in the eyes of the envious, beyond their right—and now they would be made to pay for it. Envy was being acted out, as never before.

Various reasons have been given for the extent of Jewish success, both in Europe and here in America, most of them interesting, no one, or even group, of them utterly convincing. The first of these, in chronology and also in venomousness, is the *Protocols of Zion*, which postulates an international Jewish conspiracy, Jew helping Jew in networking so elaborate and subtle as to be beyond imagining. I have heard it argued—not very persuasively—that the chief reason for Jewish success in our time is that the brightest Jews of Europe escaped, thus leaving a somewhat purified and greatly enriched gene pool from which to draw. The most common, and far from nutty, theory holds that Jews acquired savvy because, owing to prejudice against them, they had to devise other than conventional ways to succeed.

But even before Jews recorded impressive success, they were subject to a less easily formulated envy. At the center of Judaism, if not always at the center of Jewish life, is separateness. Part of the burden of being, as the Bible specified, God's "chosen people" was that Jews were to declare and maintain their separateness, which they did in myriad ways: through circumcision, through dietary laws, through hundreds of small rituals that qualified a Jew to call himself "observant."

A two-edged sword seems to be at work against the Jews: they can attempt to assimilate themselves completely in whatever society they live in—Israel, of course, excepted—for which they are likely to be despised, or they can maintain their separateness, for which they are also likely to be despised. "If assimilated," writes Frederic Raphael, in a lecture he titled "The Necessity of Anti-Semitism," "he [the Jew] becomes indistinguishable; if he insists on being indigestible, he sticks in the throat of the world." Raphael's own preference in the matter comes through, when, earlier in the lecture, he recounts the story of a minor Franco-Jewish playwright who, after the Nazis had conquered Paris and ordered Jews to wear yellow stars, wore his while driving in a fiacre, a small horse-drawn carriage, and smoking a cigar. When a friend warned him this mightn't be a good idea, he replied, "My dear fellow, this is no moment to hide one's light under a bushel."

"Everybody is someone's Jew," Primo Levi said, implying that everyone has someone he can look down upon, including, the assumption behind the statement is, the Jews themselves. But I think with the Jews there is a difference. I don't think they are merely looked down upon. Where contempt for the Jews is felt or expressed, I think that with it envy is almost always richly admixed.

Jewry is not a club out of which it is easy to get; nor, after the events of the twentieth century, would it be honorable to wish to do so. Although as a Jew I have never in any sense felt "chosen," I not infrequently have felt a special sense of privilege, even snobbish superiority at what I take to be the good luck of my having been born Jewish—and especially, let me quickly add, Jewish in America. (Had I been born Jewish in Europe—my birth date is 9 January 1937—there is a good chance I should not now be alive to write this.) Having been born in America, I am able to be both part of a great nation, and, having been born Jewish, simultaneously just a bit outside it, too. Not at all a bad position to be in, certainly for one who writes.

And yet, reversing things, what, I wonder, would I, or anyone else who is Jewish, think of the Jews if I wasn't Jewish? Would anti-Semitism creep into my thoughts, if not my conversation, if only from time to time? Would I have had enough talk of the damn Jews and their too regularly adverting to the Holocaust? Would I be slightly suspicious—and of course envious—of their landing so many good jobs in science and medicine, in academic life, in the media? Would I feel a touch of that envy that has just the slightest curl of real ugliness in it when I contemplate the successes that they and their children seem to pile up in what is coming to seem an increasingly meritocratic America? Does such behavior on the part of Jews, calculated really to do no more than make the best of life's opportunities, also, almost of necessity, incur envy?

I hope not. And yet—why not? Why shouldn't it? Envy doesn't need much in the way of excuses to begin humming and the Jews, throughout their long and complex history, but especially through their successes in the face of adversity, have offered excuses aplenty.

CHAPTER TEN

Enjoying the Fall

Envy is perhaps most coldly served when it travels between us and people we haven't met—and in fact are never likely to meet. I have in mind the celebrated, in one line of endeavor or another: athletes, film stars, famous artists, the astonishingly rich. "Our strongest, most vital hatred," wrote Paul Valéry, "goes to those who are what we would like to be ourselves; a hatred all the keener because this state is so closely wrapped up with the person whom we hate. It's a form of 'theft' to have wealth or the honors we would like to have; and it is downright murder to have the physique, brains, or gifts that are someone's ideal. For the fact of another man's possessing them shows at a glance that this ideal is not unattainable and also that the place is bespoken." How pleasing it is, then, to see these

"I'm sorry you're having a hard time, Roy. Please forgive my Schadenfreude."

people who have what we want come unraveled, fail, fall in an embarrassing, or, even better, humiliating way.

The standard, the unavoidable, question for most of us when visited by unreasonable misfortune—accidents, unearned illnesses, unfair burdens—is Why me? Why did this have to happen to me, whose life is already weighed down with sufficient difficulties? But in envy mode the question, once again, becomes, Why them? why did they have the outrageous good luck to be born athletic, beautiful, talented, wealthy? What entitles them to all that money, attention, love, easy living? Why them and why not me?

My guess is that this question was asked rather less insistently 40 or 50 years ago. Personal finances were then considered just that—personal, and hence nobody's business—whereas today it is close to common knowledge how much athletes earn per season, actors per movie, certain writers per book deal. When designers take their companies public, when CEOs leave one large company for another, when celebrities of various sorts purchase real estate, we are usually told, with some precision, how much money is entailed. Sometimes the sums are designated with painful exactitude, broken down with excruciating precision: as when one is told, say, that a major-league pitcher earns more than $46,000 per inning, or that a pop singer more than $6 million for a single night's work.

"The Houston Rockets signed point guard Steve Francis to a six-year contract extension yesterday," the *New York Times* reported on 27 August 2002, "keeping him with the team through the 2008–9 season. Francis, 25, was entering the final season of a four-year deal worth just more than $14 million. His new contract will pay him between $80 and $90 million over six years." Not easy to read that small-type item in the *Times* without one's breath catching. This is no way to begin one's morning; it tends to put vinegar in one's coffee. Although I have watched my share of professional basketball, I've never heard of Steve Francis, don't know if he is black or white, sweet natured or a human misery. But like nearly everyone else outside his immediate family I feel that he can't possibly be worth roughly $14 million dollars a year for wearing shorts and bouncing a round rubbery ball up and down a basketball court. Already, without knowing anything about him, I'm pretty certain I do not like this guy. I hope his family will forgive me, but I'm not sure I altogether wish him well.

In an earlier time, too, we did not know the rich and famous as well as we feel we know them now. Cary Grant and Rita Hayworth did not go on television talk shows to expose their possible ignorance. Babe Ruth and Sonja Henie did not submit to intimate profiles in slick magazines. Public relations firms were then employed not to bring publicity to the very wealthy but to keep them out of publicity's glare. And a good thing they did, if only to ward off envy.

No longer. Now we know how much the glamorous and oddly talented earn and what they are like. One response to this knowledge is to feel the injustice of it all and to go on from there to despise them, at least a little. Many people, I believe, do comfortably despise them. Certainly enough do so to make possible the American version of the English gutter press, our grocery press, *The National Enquirer, The Globe*, the New York tabloids, and the rest, whose central job, it seems to me, is to satisfy envy by displaying, at every opportunity, the talented, the famous, and the wealthy in one or another stage of defeat.

The grocery-gutter press, which might also be called *The National Schadenfreude*, trumpets in its headlines: Oprah has gained 60 pounds while binge feeding. Britney Spears's boyfriend is cheating on her. Cher's daughter is in deep trouble. Brad Pitt is making a mess of his marriage. Whitney Houston hasn't licked her drug problems. Another of the Kennedy grandchildren has done something disgraceful. Donald Trump is being hauled into court for still higher alimony. The score is evening out and the world is a more just place than one might at first have thought. As Jackie Gleason's comic character Ralph Kramden used to exclaim, "How sweet it is!"

Schadenfreude is the emotion that is in operation here: delight in another's failure or defeat. *Schadenfreude* has a long history—as long, some might say, as the history of human nature. Jonathan Swift, in the seventeenth century, sensed that it might apply to himself, when he wrote "Verses on the Death of Dr. Swift," with a couplet about others learning of his death that runs: "They hug themselves, and reason thus: It is not yet so bad with us." Swift also recognized how philosophically we are all able to take the misfortune of the next person:

> Indifference clad in wisdom's guise
> All fortitude of mind supplies.

Schadenfreude is scarcely a new and is more likely an age-old phenomenon—a hardy perennial in the weedy garden of sour emotions. Lord Byron saw it in operation behind the attacks on the playwright and politician Richard Sheridan, and described it thus:

> The secret enemy whose sleepless eye
> Stands sentimental, accuser, judge and spy,
> The foe, the fool, the jealous and the vain,
> The envious who but breathe in others' pain.
> Behold the host, delighting to deprave,
> Who traces the steps of glory to the grave,
> Watch every fault that daring genius owes
> Half to the ardour which its birth bestows,
> Distort the truth, accumulate the lie,
> And pile the pyramid of calumny.

Nothing seems to bring *Schadenfreude* out more vigorously than the spectacle of the mighty fallen. (In the political realm, the journalist Andrew Sullivan coined the term "yankenfreude" to describe European pleasure at American economic woes.) Sometimes, let it be said, the mighty really do deserve to fall, and something other than *Schadenfreude* is entailed: one thinks here of the corporate capers attempted at Enron, WorldCom, and at other corporations whose deep corruption was glaringly revealed. Here less envy than a sense of justice enters in. The upper echelon executives whose kites crashed are characters who lied, cheated, evaded all responsibility, looked out exclusively for themselves, and told their employees, in effect, to go screw themselves. Not envy but contempt was the chief emotion felt in wanting to see them fall, and for most people they haven't yet fallen far enough. This isn't, I think, *Schadenfreude* but, more simply, a genuine hunger for justice.

And what of Martha Stewart, whose crime was to heed an insider stock tip and unload a large wad of stock before its price plummeted? Vast segments of the country seemed pleased—make that delighted—when she was, in effect, caught in the act. The Internet at the time was alight with *Martha* magazines that showed her behind bars, offering tips on cell decoration and hints on all the charming things that might be done with prison stripes. Was the pleasure in Martha Stewart's fall justified, or tinged with—make that propelled by—*Schadenfreude?*

My guess is that it is the latter. Here is a woman, Martha Stewart, who made an enormous sum of money by telling everyone how they ought to conduct the domestic details of their lives, who suddenly turns up to have some rather sordid details in her own domestic-financial life. (The crime of accepting insider stock information is one of which, I dare say, most of us would not like to be put to the test.) Martha Stewart is not among Swiss Family Epstein's household gods, but I know enough about her to have felt a fluttering of not very intense but still quite real *Schadenfreude* of my own at her fall.

Sometimes the distinction between *Schadenfreude* and justice hunger is a tough call. I recall learning of cancer having been found in a literary critic who always claimed something close to moral perfection for himself. I recall telling this to my wife, adding that, moral prig though I thought him, I didn't wish him to die. My wife, who had no real stake in the subject, allowed as how she understood, and told me that she knew that I merely wished him more stress in his life. Exactly, more stress: a frightening letter from the IRS, his third marriage to go sour, his children to express an intense distaste for his world-view—not death but stress. This man had won prizes, professorships, heavy (and I thought undeserved) esteem from the world, that great ninny, certainly much more than I had won. Was what I felt for him anchored in envy or was it good clean dislike for someone authentically fraudulent? Naturally, I prefer to think the latter, but I wish I could be more confident that envy had nothing to do with it.

Some psychologists believe that *Schadenfreude* is fueled chiefly by envy. They run so-called controlled experiments in which, generally, the people whose failure is most enthusiastically appreciated are those who seemed to come by their gifts without the least effort. The naturally bright, the astonishingly well coordinated, the flawlessly beautiful—these are the people the envious prefer to see crash and burn.

Some people feel *Schadenfreude* heartily and speak of it openly; others secretly luxuriate in it; and still others feel it guiltily. Should one feel guilt along with what *Schadenfreude* one feels, however intense or fleeting? Probably. Surely it is intrinsically wrong to wish to see people cursed because they also happen to have been blessed with gifts greater than one's own. The psychologists of *Schadenfreude* tend to believe that those who feel it most strongly are likely to be people who do not have a good opinion of themselves and thus exult unduly in watching other people dragged down. Still, to enjoy, if only mildly, the fall of the high placed, seems rather a natural if unpleasant part of human nature.

What seems less natural is (secretly) enjoying the defeat of acquaintances, friends, even family. La Rochefoucauld, who not only didn't mind gazing into the darker side of human nature but made his name by italicizing it through the formulation of his splendid maxims, has two maxims bearing directly on this point: "Nous avons tous assez de force pour supporter les maux d'autris" ("We all have strength enough to endure the misfortunes of others") and "Nous consoler aisement disgraces de nos amis lorsquell' elles servent a signaler a notre tendresse pour eux" ("We are easily consoled for the misfortunes of our friends, if they afford us an opportunity for displaying our affections.") The latter maxim supplies the best reason I know why one does well never to let someone who offers to do so speak at a memorial for someone you love.

Schadenfreude in connection with the distantly famous is one thing; the same delight at the disappointments of people nearer to one, not precluding those whom one is supposed to care about, even love, is quite another. From envy at the success of one's friends—Gore Vidal writes: "Whenever a friend succeeds, a little something in me dies"—to genuine pleasure at their failure is a decisive step downward. The feeling of quiet satisfaction accompanying the failure to rise of a decent but perhaps overly ambitious friend; the quiet delight in seeing foiled the educational plans for the children of cousins who have put too much hope in getting them in the very best schools; the suppressed joy in watching even one's own sister's hope for a more elegant way of living squelched—ah, now we come to envy with real bite to it. We come to the place where envy, turning up in the form of *Schadenfreude*, really does begin to seem a sin, yes, by God, a seriously deadly one.

CHAPTER ELEVEN

Resentment by Any Other Name

Some psychologists believe that not envy but resentment is the major force behind *Schadenfreude*. But resentment itself is also often behind envy, and the similarities and distinctions between these two states of mind need to be made clear. People who specialize in making them, in fact, begin by tossing out the word "resentment" and replacing it with the French version, *ressentiment*.

Their reason for doing so is that resentment can be a quick, stabbing thing, set off by an act of ingratitude or injustice, but that can, fairly quickly, melt away. Envy usually has a specific object, and should it be obtained, then envy itself is put to rest. The same

is true of revenge: once it is acquired, the books are closed. But *ressentiment* is of greater endurance, has a way of insinuating itself into personality, becoming a permanent part of one's character.

The great thinker on the subject, author of the book *Ressentiment,* is Max Scheler (1874–1928). In his view, *ressentiment* begins in a feeling of impotence. *Ressentiment* is more passive than straight envy. When one knows one cannot alter a situation one doesn't like, but cannot quite resign oneself to it, *ressentiment* is often the result. Under *ressentiment* one undervalues and thereby degrades the thing one cannot do or have or equal. The key *ressentiment* story, as various commentators have pointed out, is that of Aesop's "The Fox and the Grapes." Since the fox cannot reach the grapes anyhow, he concludes that they must not be any good—pure *ressentiment*—and so says the hell with them.

"Instead of defining the word [*ressentiment*]," Scheler writes, "let us briefly characterize the phenomenon. *Ressentiment* is a self-poisoning of the mind which has quite definite causes and consequences. It is a lasting mental attitude, caused by the systematic regression of certain emotions and affects which, as such, are normal components of human nature. Their repression leads to the constant tendency to indulge in certain kinds of value delusions and corresponding value judgments. The emotions and affects primarily concerned are revenge, hatred, malice, envy, the impulse to detract, and spite."

Ressentiment, then, is a state of mind, one that leaves those it possesses with a general feeling of grudgingness toward life. Those who suffer from it, feeling their impotence, do not believe that much if anything can be done about the source of their resentful feelings. Scheler believed that *ressentiment* could "only arise if these emotions are particularly powerful and yet must be suppressed because they are coupled with the feeling that one is unable to act them out—either because of weakness, physical or mental, or because of fear." This frequently ends, according to Scheler, in "embittering" and "poisoning" the personality. So much so that those suffering *ressentiment* come almost to enjoy the occasions for criticism that their outlook allows them. Criticism propelled by *ressentiment* does not expect, or even look forward to, the eradication of what it considers wrong, or bad, or evil; without these flaws and faults, "the growing pleasure afforded by invective and negation" would be destroyed.

Scheler underscores again and again that the element of impotence is what makes for *ressentiment*. Envy, hatred, the need for revenge end in *ressentiment* only when one knows one can do nothing about them. Thus for Scheler, criminals, who feel no impotence—except perhaps after being caught and locked away— suffer no *ressentiment*. Nor are soldiers likely to feel it. Until recent decades, many women felt it, at least socially and occupationally, but perhaps now, in the wake of feminism's political victories, *ressentiment* has been displaced by other problems and difficulties. The aged can easily lapse into a *ressentiment* group: "No wonder," Scheler writes, "that youth always has a hard fight to sustain against the *ressentiment* of the aged." Mothers-in-law are another collective *ressentiment*-suffering group Scheler cites—once so powerfully in control of their children, mothers-in-law, after their children marry, are generally shucked of all power, left only with sullen resentment.

Different groups will be saturated by *ressentiment* at different times. If the proletariat may once have felt the impotence of powerlessness, at least in Karl Marx's imagining of their condition, labor unions and their rise under twentieth-century capitalism seem to have put an end to it. Some artists, feeling undervalued in a philistine society, have known and shown *ressentiment*. American veterans of the Vietnam War have, I think, long suffered serious *ressentiment*, though many would say for just reasons: they are impotent in making clear the importance of their sacrifices, given the apparently permanent ambiguity that most Americans feel about the Vietnam War.

My own candidate for a large group existing in a state of *ressentiment* would be American academics, especially those in the humanities. They feel themselves, simultaneously, greatly superior and vastly undervalued, above their countrymen yet isolated from them and insufficiently rewarded and revered by them.

They have about them a perpetually disappointed air: one senses they feel that the world has, somehow, let them down. Sometimes this will reveal itself in a general sourness; sometimes it takes the form of hopelessly radical political views. These political views, it does not take long to recognize, usually feature a complex shifting and reorientation of society so that people like themselves will be allowed a justly deserved role of power.

The best account for the *ressentiment* of American academics that I've seen is one presented by the philosopher Robert Nozick. His view was that university teachers were almost invariably people who, because of their superior performance in school, were told over and over again how bright and extraordinary they are. This continued for 20 years—from grade through graduate school—with sufficient reinforcement, that is, for them to be convinced of its truth. They remain in the environment, that of the classroom, that has long been the scene of all their rewards, by becoming teachers.

It all seems like a good life, but soon it is spoiled by the realization that people who did less well than they in school seem to be faring rather better in the world. Not quite first-class lawyers are making hundreds of thousands of dollars a year; dullish boys and girls, now practicing medicine, have large summer homes near gentle lakes. Coarse creeps are scoring heavily in the stock and commodities markets. While they, once the darlings of their teachers—who bestowed all those lovely A's upon them—are struggling along, not only financially but spiritually. No, it's not working out at all, and it's damn unfair.

Originally, an unwritten contract of a sort was made. Through teaching and the university life, it was understood, one would be allowed to indulge one's intellectual and artistic passions in exchange for denying oneself the heavy luxuries of life available to others out battling in the marketplace. But it hasn't quite played out as planned. Teaching turns out to be less exhilarating than promised. Those brilliant books one had hoped to write haven't got done. One's students refuse to demonstrate a passion for the life of the mind worthy of one's own. The leisure that teaching allows is as advertised, but the pay really isn't quite adequate; certainly it doesn't allow one to live up to one's own high state of cultivation. Why does some ignorant lawyer have enough money to buy a villa in Tuscany when one knows so much much more about the art of the Italian Renaissance? What kind of society permits this state of things to exist? A seriously unjust one, that's what kind.

And so envy mixes with snobbery, with impotence added, all mounted against a background of cosmic injustice, to put a large class of persons into a permanent condition of *ressentiment*.

Max Scheler enlarges the scope of *ressentiment* when he claims that "the core of bourgeois morality, which gradually replaced Christian morality ever since the 13th century and culminated in the French Revolution, is rooted in *ressentiment.*" Was *ressentiment*, that peculiar combination of envy and impotence, what the rising bourgeois chiefly felt when he encountered nobility? I'm not prepared to say, but I do know that, at one time or another in our lives, nearly all of us have felt this discouraging and debilitating emotion, conferring the dark and heavy feeling of hopelessness made permanent.

CHAPTER TWELVE

Is Envying Human Nature?

Some cultures are more pervaded by envy than others. If it is true that envy is felt more strongly between near equals than between those widely separated in fortune—it doesn't really seem to make much sense, does it, to envy the Queen of England?—then democratic republics ought to provide the most active arenas for envy. And often they do. America qualifies here in various ways. Alexis de Tocqueville—the unavoidable Tocqueville—noted that "democratic institutions most successfully develop sentiments of envy in the human heart."

As I earlier mentioned, envy may never have had such free reign with such brutal consequences as in the Soviet Union, with its official commitment to the dictatorship of the proletariat and to universal brotherhood. Dismaying though it is to report, another culture in which envy played a central role is that of the most admired of all cultures in Western history, the Greeks, and especially in Athens, in the fifth and fourth centuries B.C. In his brief but excellent book *Envy and The Greeks*, Peter Walcot writes: "The very fact that one is successful and prosperous . . . is a good enough reason for the Greeks why one should be envied. To have done someone a wrong is another reason why one should be disliked and subject to malice and envy. . . . Envy [among the Greeks] is a fact of life rather than a moral principle." Again and again Walcot underscores that "the Greeks were acutely aware of the problem, and they at least faced up to it fearlessly, acknowledging that man was envious and making no attempt to suppress the unpalatable fact that envy was manifest everywhere." The heavily militarized city-state of Sparta made the most strenuous attempt to set up an envy-free polis, with a common mess at which all ate their meals together and by removing children from their parents and raising them in a communitarian way.

"Man, according to the Greeks, is naturally envious, envy being part of his basic character and disposition," writes Walcot, who goes on to show that envy in Greek life took various forms, among siblings, among peers, between the common and the prominent citizens. As if this weren't enough, the Greeks also worried about the the envy of the gods. Implicit in the Greek fear of invoking the envy of the gods was the idea that not alone hubris (that ample pride that goes before that total fall) but mere prosperity could arouse their wrath.

Many of us have inherited some of these same views, even if we do not speak of gods. Although we know ourselves to be living in the twenty-first century, we are still, in various *sub rosa* ways, attempting to ward off envy. When things go well for me, I am often rendered slightly nervous that they might be going too well and that, with justice's tendency to right things, I shall be made to pay for my small successes with much greater defeats. In a world with so much sadness, after all, why should I be blessed with too regular a supply of good fortune? Hubris must be warded off; I must remind myself, over and over, how rare is my luck. I must express my gratitude, recalling that W. H. Auden used to say that the begging part of prayer should be got over quickly so that one can go directly to the thanking and gratitude part.

What made the Greeks different, according to Peter Walcot, was that they, in effect, institutionalized ways of dealing with envy. They did not think for a moment they could suppress envy, but instead invented ways of giving vent to it and, where possible, making it slightly less noxious.

The political institution of ostracism, for example, by which a political leader could be removed from office, was often regarded as a means of reducing the envy felt for him. The most famous—and perhaps most sad—case of ostracism in Greek history was that of the Greek statesman Aristides the Just, whom, Plutarch reports, was ostracized because of an excess virtue, if virtue can ever be said to suffer from an excess. "I'm fed up with hearing him called the Just everywhere," an Athenian citizen is supposed to have remarked. (A case could be made that Socrates was not ostracized but condemned to death for the same reason— envy of his great virtue and complete integrity.) The admiral and statesman Themistocles also suffered ostracism, in his case for living beyond the democratic norm and having been thought to take on superior airs.

Ostracism meant a ten-year exile, but without loss of citizenship or property. Anyone put through ostracism was permitted to return, and indeed it was expected that he would do so. But his ostracism, meanwhile, allowed him, in a phrase of our day, to cool it. The envy felt for him would have time to abate.

Everywhere in Greek society there was the tension between natural competition and the bar of rising too high above one's fellow citizens. This explains why, so often when one reads about the victories of Greeks in athletic or other competitions, the winner is to be found distributing lavish gifts to the citizenry, lest he incur too intense a swell of envy for his good fortune. Envy was viewed by the Greeks as empty-headed, wrong, a wretched habit that could come to dominate one's character. But the Greeks' understanding it so did not mean they thought it could be abolished. The best hope was that it could be dealt with and perhaps diminished. The Greeks took envy to be part of human nature, running at differing intensities in differing people, but always there, ever ready to emerge, like a coiled snake, seemingly asleep but easily stirred into poisonous attack.

Christians, being more reformed-minded, thought they could root out envy. "Love does not envy," said St. Paul, and so the problem was, seemingly, simplified: love thy neighbor, even thy enemy. Jesus among his apostles attempted to root out envy by rooting out its arch cause: rivalry. Jesus attempted to convince all that earthly rewards are at best minor rewards. Glory, riches, power were as nothing compared to what was on offer in the world beyond. The prize on which one must keep one's eye is that of heaven, next to which all else isn't even trivial.

Behind the Christian view on envy is the hope, through spreading the doctrine of Christ, to establish a utopia here on earth in which envy will simply have no place. Christian or not, everyone must decide for him- or herself how realistic this is; one must decide, finally, whether envy is or is not part of human nature. If it's not, it can perhaps be shorn from us all. If it is a part of human nature, as Aristotle and the other Greek philosophers thought it was, then the problem becomes one of damage control. How best can we keep it contained?

Alas, it appears to be a question without, just now, an answer. For all our progress in science and invention, the two things we remain in darkness about are how the mind works and what constitutes human nature. Paul McHugh, a neurologist and until recently head of psychiatry at Johns Hopkins, has said that, in the study of the mind, such is our ignorance that we haven't even come as far as physiologists did when William Harvey, in the seventeenth century, discovered the circulation of the blood. In other words, we don't know even the most fundamental mechanisms of the mind and its operations. Without such knowledge, we can only poke about, and assign to men and women a human nature that is in accord with our personal experience, our politics, our cheerfulness or want of cheerfulness. We add to this bits of psychology, social science, general reading, and conclude, or at least some people do, that men and women are "naturally" this or that, ranging from exquisite *homo sapiens* to brutish *homo rapiens*. But when we talk about human nature—and who can help talking about it?—we are really dancing, cheek to cheek, in the dark. The Greeks, in assuming that, whatever human nature might be, envy was surely a part of it, may have been wiser than we.

CHAPTER THIRTEEN

Professional Envy

The first place to look for envy is of course in one's own heart. I have known a good deal of envy over more than six decades of life, but perhaps never more than when I was a boy. That mine was a reasonably happy childhood did not prevent me from wanting it to be happier still, and the quickest way to this happiness seemed to be to possess some of those things that other boys had that I didn't. I do not recall envying girls. I can remember, before I was ten years old, envying boys who were better looking, better coordinated, with wealthier parents, brighter, more popular, and more physically courageous than I. And this was just among my contemporaries. I even mildly envied Catholics; growing up in the heavily Catholic city of Chicago at a time when every other movie

"Damn it with faint praise."

seemed to star Bing Crosby or Pat O'Brien or Barry Fitzgerald playing charming priests, to be Catholic seemed to me to be American to the highest power.

As I grew into adolescence, the repertoire of my envy grew, becoming wider but also deeper. I envied boys who were more attractive to girls than I; boys who were better athletes; boys who seemed more adept and more at ease in the world. I also felt my first stabs of jealousy, having at one point a cute but flirtatious girlfriend. Jealousy allowed for an imagined drama—there was scarcely anyone I could not imagine her betraying me with—and gave my mind something to brood upon. My feelings of envy were quite different: less concentrated, more vaporous yet somehow more pervasive.

I cannot say that I was, in the cliché formulation, consumed by envy, but it was there, usually cropping up in smaller matters than in large. I had lots of freedom, but I knew boys who had more and, with it, more pocket money than I, which redoubled their freedom. I read a number of what I supposed should be called juvenile delinquency novels— *The Amboy Dukes, A Stone for Danny Fisher, Knock on Any Door, The Hoods*—and came away from them envying a lower-class upbringing, which, if these novels were to be believed, seemed to make for more abundant and readily available sex. In my adolescence, almost nothing in the atmosphere did not seem enviable, from the possession of prominent biceps to Tony Curtis's hairdo.

If my envy was fairly constant, none of it was intense; most of it was fairly normal. When young one tends to imagine those one envies as, somehow, luckier than oneself. Then, too, when young, one is less than clear what is important in one's life, and therefore one's wants tend to be almost endless. One wants the large house in the rich suburb one drives through; one wants the love of the pretty cheerleader with whom one has never spoken; one wants the flashy car, the elegant clothes, the swell suntan even—one wants, wants, wants, and all this wanting opens one up to a generalized envy.

My envy only took on particularity when I decided that I wanted to be a writer. This put me in an immediate position to envy other writers of my generation who, in the way the world measured such things, had advanced more quickly than I. In my twenties, I recall reading in the contributors notes of *Poetry Magazine* that a woman with three poems in the current issue had been born two years after me, which was enough to ruin my day— and I didn't even desire to write poetry. The notion of people my age or younger having written books, some of them quite good books, was more than upsetting. I did not precisely want them to die, but, wondering why they hadn't the simple courtesy to allow my achievements to be recognized first, I wanted them, somehow, stopped. The moral of this little story, I believe, is that it is difficult to be ambitious without also being envious.

Professional achievement, I noticed, seemed to bring out intramural envy. For many years the three best art critics in America didn't speak to one another. I have been around immensely successful novelists who couldn't abide the success of other, even much lesser novelists. ("I don't know how it is in other professions," a character in George Gissing's novel *New Grub Street* says, "but I hope there is less envy, hatred, and malice than in ours.") Poets, having the smallest literary audience in our day, may be the most recklessly envious of all the workers in the arts, thought I have heard it said that musical performers, with larger audiences, also do quite a good job in this line. I recently read that Koussevitsky gave lots of conducting work at the Boston Symphony to Igor Stravinsky, because he felt "a composer-conductor" was not a genuine rival to a full-time conductor.

Envy only takes on a poisonous quality when it hits a certain level of intensity or when one still everywhere feels it at a time when one has reached an age that ought to have allowed one to put it well to the side. I have disliked, despised, felt contempt for, and even (temporarily) hated several people over my lifetime, but have I ever envied anyone with the kind of poisonous strength that genuine envy entails? I hope I am telling the truth when I say that I don't think I have. But even now stabs of envy— hopeless, foolish envy—still affect me, who is of an age to know better. "Malice may be sometimes out of breath," wrote Lord Halifax, "envy never."

CHAPTER FOURTEEN

Poor Mental Hygiene

I have never known life without desire," remarks Zeno, the hero of Italo Svevo's novel *The Confessions of Zeno*, and neither have I. Even today, I enter a grand house and cannot help thinking about owning it. I see a dazzling car and imagine myself driving it along the ocean. Some poet or novelist is awarded a vast stash of prize money, and I think, it will not shock you to learn, how much worthier of the dough am I than he. Paul Valéry, the lucidity and depth of whose mind I shall never cease to envy, once wrote about seeing someone "in a light that causes him to seem so happy or so handsome that it makes us lose even the taste for living," and I know that feeling, too. But none of these little tremors of envy seems to have any real staying power. They are closer to fleeting fantasy than genuine envy. Nowadays reality kicks in too quickly—I think of the cost of maintaining a grand house (landscaping, heating bills, taxes), the inconvenience of a convertible in winter, the low characters who have won the grandest literary prizes—and my envy deflates, with the same flatulent noise of air leaving a balloon.

I have, moreover, become resigned to my middling station in life. I want only a genteel sufficiency of lolly to live without fear of debt or having to stint too greatly on myself and especially on those I love. I have had enough of the world's honors and, while I have an astonishingly high threshold for praise, I find I can carry on well enough without a regular supply of tributes, kudos, and awards. I've not accumulated all that much wisdom, but I have come to know that the world, in its judgments of achievement, hasn't shown great accuracy, and so without too much anguish can accept its negligence in not fully recognizing my talent.

I feel myself extremely lucky in finding the right work, the right friends, above all in my wife the right partner in life. A man who feels himself lucky also feels—or at any rate ought to feel—the unseemliness of relentless envy. Yet even the lucky continue to feel spurts of envy. Some years ago I wrote an essay called "A Few Kind Words for Envy," which ended with a list of the things that I still envied. Only one expensive item was on the list: a small well-made house with a fine view of water. The rest were both priceless and, at this point in my life, unattainable. As I said then, I envied anyone who could do a backward somersault in midair from a standing position. I envied people who had fought in a war, had their bravery tested, and come through intact. I envied people who spoke foreign languages easily. I envied performing artists of various kinds who can enthrall an audience to the point where the audience doesn't want the performance ever to end. I envied people who can travel abroad with a single piece of luggage. I envied people who have exceedingly good posture. I still envy such people. And, above all, I envied—and continue to envy—those few people, favorites of the gods, who genuinely understand that life is a fragile bargain, rescindable at any time by another party (who shall be nameless), and live their lives— day by day, hour by hour, minute by minute—accordingly.

Whatever else it is, Envy is above all a great waste of mental energy. While it cannot be proved whether or not envy is part of human nature, what can be proven, I believe, is that, unleashed, envy tends to diminish all in whom it takes possession. Wherever envy comes into play, judgment is coarsened and cheapened. However the mind works, envy, we know, is one of its excesses, and as such it must be identified and fought against by the only means at our disposal: self-honesty, self-analysis, and balanced judgment.

If theological thinking is unavailable to you, if the very notion of "sin," original or unoriginal, as damning simply makes no sense to you, I would invite you instead to consider envy less as a sin than as very poor mental hygiene. It blocks out clarity, both about oneself and the people one envies, and it ends by giving one a poor opinion of oneself. No one can see clearly anything he or she envies. Envy clouds thought, clobbers generosity, precludes any hope of serenity, and ends in shriveling the heart—reasons enough to fight free of it with all one's mental strength.

A Bibliographic Note

The social scientific literature of envy is not a rich one, owing chiefly to the fact that the sin—vice? condition? quality?—of envy is not one about which people are likely to be forthcoming. This point and others are made in *The Psychology of Jealousy and Envy* edited by Peter Salovey. One very useful book devoted entirely to the subject is Helmut Schoeck's *Envy: A Theory of Social Behavior.* A great German meal of a book, Schoeck's is a heavy but highly nourishing work that touches on every aspect of its subject and is indispensable to anyone who writes on this rich but complex matter.

Envy is, inevitably, a chapter or two in books devoted to the seven deadly sins. Two such books that I found useful, and amusing, are Ian Fleming's edited compilation on the seven deadly sins and the English journalist Henry Fairlie's updating of the seven deadlies. A more scholarly approach to the subject is available in Harold Bloomfield's study, *The Seven Deadly Sins,* whose subtitle gives a vivid enough sense of its weight and tone: "An Introduction to the History of a Religious Concept, with Special Reference to Medieval English Literature."

Envy is a subject that plays in and out of literature. *Billy Budd, Sailor,* is perhaps the greatest single work devoted to the subject in a concentrated way. Envy pops up from time to time in Shakespeare, but then, in that most universal of writers, what doesn't? I make mention in the foregoing pages of a novel written under the iron heel of the Soviet Union, perhaps the most envy-laden country in the history of the world, and of the dystopian novel *Facial Justice* by L. P. Hartley. Envy is a note sounded strongly in a number of the poems of Philip Larkin, a poet in whom the note of yearning (the innocent cousin to envy) also resoundingly sounds.

The French *moralistes* could scarcely be said to exist without envy, and though La Rochefoucauld is the only one I quote, La Bruyere, Chamfort, and Vauvenargues would all but be out of business without envy. So would have the Duc de Saint-Simon, great chronicler of the court of Louis XIV, which may be said to have run on pomp and envy.

Envy is a subject that any philosopher even distantly interested in human nature must ineluctably touch upon. I quote or refer only to Aristotle, Kant, Kierkegaard, Schopenhauer, Nietsche, and John Rawls in these pages, but more extensive reading is likely to discover other philosophers with genuine insight on the subject.

Mine is a book only partly built upon other books. Much more of its material comes from simply living in the world and looking about. Even more, it derives from gazing into my own heart, which has never for long, alas, been entirely envy-free.

Here is a partial list of some of the main books I consulted in writing my own book:

Aristotle, *Rhetoric, Nicomachean Ethics*

Bacon, Francis, *Essays*

Bloomfield, Harold, *The Seven Deadly Sins*

Fairlie, Henry, *The Seven Deadly Sins Today*

Farber, Leslie, *Lying, Despair, Jealousy, Envy, Sex, Suicide, Drugs, and the Good Life*

Fleming, Ian (editor), *The Seven Deadly Sins*

Frank, Robert H., *Luxury Fever*

Freud, Sigmund, *The Interpretation of Dreams, Collected Papers*

Hartley, L. P., *Facial Justice*

Kant, Immanuel, *The Metaphysics of Morals*

Kierkegaard, Sören, *Fear and Trembling, The Sickness onto Death*

Klein, Melanie, *Envy and Gratitude and Other Works*

Larkin, Philip, *Collected Poems*

La Rochefoucauld, *Maximes*

Matt, Susan J., *Keeping Up with the Joneses: Envy in American Consumer Society, 1890–1930*

Melville, Herman, *Great Short Works of Herman Melville*

Nietzsche, Friedrich, *All Too Human, The Gay Science*

Olesha, Y. *Envy, A Novel*

Portman, John, *When Bad Things Happen to Other People*

Rawls, John, *Theory of Justice*

Salovey, Peter (editor), *The Psychology of Jealousy and Envy*

Scheler, Max, *Ressentiment*

Schoeck, Helmut, *Envy: A Theory of Social Behavior*

Schopenhauer, Arthur, *Complete Essays of Schopenhauer*

Walcot, Peter, *Envy and The Greeks*

Index